OECD Public Governance Reviews

I0126130

Engaging Citizens in Jordan's Local Government Needs Assessment Process

OECD

This document, as well as any data and map included herein, are without prejudice to the status of or sovereignty over any territory, to the delimitation of international frontiers and boundaries and to the name of any territory, city or area.

Please cite this publication as:
OECD (2020), *Engaging Citizens in Jordan's Local Government Needs Assessment Process*, OECD Public Governance Reviews, OECD Publishing, Paris, *https://doi.org/10.1787/c3bddbcb-en*.

ISBN 978-92-64-52125-4 (print)
ISBN 978-92-64-81147-8 (pdf)

OECD Public Governance Reviews
ISSN 2219-0406 (print)
ISSN 2219-0414 (online)

Foreword

Local governments – regional, provincial, and municipal –have a direct impact on people's daily lives and are essential to building more open and inclusive societies. Not only are local governments often responsible for the delivery of crucial services, but they also play an intermediary role between public and national administrations. Given their proximity to citizens, they are often more present, and have a better understanding of public priorities and of differences in needs. Implementing reforms at the local level may therefore offer the greatest opportunity to transform the relationship between the government and its citizens by providing meaningful and direct opportunities to participate in public life.

Acknowledging these benefits, Jordan has committed to placing citizens at the heart of its ongoing decentralization reform process. Following the enactment of its decentralization laws in 2015, Jordan has embarked on a process to shift development decisions to the governorate, municipal and local levels. This reform has introduced a bottom-up approach to local planning and socio-economic development by ensuring that citizens play a larger role in identifying needs.

While progress has been achieved, the promise of decentralization in Jordan has yet to meet citizens' expectations. Indeed, the decentralization reform is taking place within – and in response to – challenging circumstances, including the COVID-19 pandemic, stagnant economic growth, and strained service delivery. To this end, leveraging the present momentum for reform with the new draft Local Administration Law will be all the more important to bring local governments closer to citizens.

At the request of the Government of Jordan, this review examines the current governance and stakeholder participation gaps in the needs assessment and development planning process. It is part of the OECD's broader work with the country on open government, gender equality and youth engagement in the framework of the MENA-OECD Governance Programme. Building on findings and recommendations from the OECD Report "Towards a New Partnership with Citizens: Jordan's Decentralisation Reform" (2017), it offers recommendations to supports the country's ambitious decentralization reform agenda. Together with the document "Supporting Open Government at the Local Level in Jordan", this work will help Jordan foster a culture of open government across levels of the administration and engage all stakeholders beyond the usual suspects.

Acknowledgements

The review was prepared by the Directorate for Public Governance (GOV) under the leadership of its former Acting Head and current Deputy Director, Janos Bertok. It is part of a long-standing collaboration with Jordan on open government, gender equality and youth engagement in the framework of the MENA-OECD Governance Programme.

The review was produced by the Open and Innovative Government Division (OIG) under the strategic direction of Alessandro Bellantoni, Head of the Open Government Unit.

The report was drafted by Craig Matasick and Paulina López Ramos with contributions from Michael Jelenic and Carla Musi. Sophie Le Corre and Elena Martin Gomez-Tembleque provided administrative support throughout the development of the publication.

The OECD Secretariat wishes to express its gratitude to all those who made the OECD Report "*Engaging Citizens in Jordan's Local Government Needs Assessment Process*" possible, especially the Government of Jordan. In particular, the OECD would like to thank the team of the Ministry of Planning and International Co-operation (MoPIC) in Jordan headed by Hatem Habahbeh. The team would also like to thank the Ministry of Local Administration, Ministry of Interior, Ministry of Finance and the Institutional Performance Development Unit at the Prime Minister's Office for their contributions to the publication. These in-depth insights were instrumental in further improving the OECD's understanding of the Jordanian context and helping to recommend courses of action that reflect local priorities. Likewise, the OECD would also like to express its appreciation for the contributions of Dr. Amer Bani's team in Al Hayat RASED.

Finally, the OECD also wishes to acknowledge the co-operation and support of the current Minister of MoPIC, Nasser Shraideh, as well as the former Minister, Wissam Rabadi, in addition to the important contributions provided by the many stakeholders from the public sector and civil society, through surveys conducted by the OECD and contributions in fact finding missions in February and March 2019[1].

---

[1] Stakeholders included elected members of governorate and municipal councils, mayors as well as officials from development units at all three levels from: The Amman Governorate; Madaba Governorate; Zarka Governorate; Mafraq Governorate; Tafilah Governorate; Ma'an Governorate; Jerash Governorate; Ajloun Governorate; Tafila Municipality; Battir District; Salt Municipality; Ajloun Municipality; Jaresh Municipality; Zarka Municipality Mafraq; Participants from civil society included representatives from: Rasheed; Opinions without borders for sustainable development; Community Media Network; Qudurat Association for Community Development; Change agents for sustainable development; Virtue Charity Association; Jordan Legal Network; We Rise Center; Tomorrow's Youth Center; Namaa Development and Capacity Building; Bashayer Al Nour Charity Associatiom; Madaba Tomorrow for development and training; Our Children's Future Cultural Association; The Creatives Association to support students and the local community; Sons of Al Khalil Association for solidarity; and Ain Rasun Charity Association.

Table of contents

Tables

Figures

Boxes

Follow OECD Publications on:

http://twitter.com/OECD_Pubs

http://www.facebook.com/OECDPublications

http://www.linkedin.com/groups/OECD-Publications-4645871

http://www.youtube.com/oecdilibrary

http://www.oecd.org/oecddirect/

Executive Summary

Since 2015, the Government of Jordan embarked on an ambitious process to decentralize power to the sub-national level in efforts to place citizens at the heart of policies and services. This impetus for reform stemmed from King Abdullah II's vision emphasizing that "political development should start at the grassroots level". In response, the enactment of the 2015 decentralization laws introduced new elected and non-elected councils at the governorate level and a participatory approach for the design of local development plans, through a yearly collection and assessment of citizens' needs, known as the "needs assessment process".

Acknowledging decentralization as an ongoing process, the Government of Jordan is continuing its efforts toward mainstreaming open government initiatives at the sub-national level to realise the promises of this historical reform. While much has been achieved with local elections in 2017 and two rounds of the needs assessment process, challenges remain to achieve a real devolution of power and meaningfully engage stakeholders in local policies. At the same time, these transformations are taking place at a volatile time for the country, with stagnating economic growth, growing perceptions of corruption, and large influxes of refugees, all of which are exacerbated by the ongoing COVID-19 pandemic.

This report analyses the main opportunities and challenges in the needs assessment process. It begins by contextualizing the factors shaping the country's decentralization reform, its main tenants and the progress achieved since the enactment of the 2015 laws (Chapter 1). The report then examines the evolution of decentralized structures at the local level and provides recommendations regarding roles and responsibilities, coordination mechanisms, strategic planning and human and financial resources (Chapter 2). The report also provides recommendations on how to better inform, communicate with, consult and engage stakeholders in the different stages of the needs assessment process (Chapters 3 and 4). Throughout, the report draws on successes from OECD member countries to illustrate good practices in this field.

Good governance enablers in the needs assessment process

Reforms to the role of sub-national governments in Jordan have raised a series of operational issues in terms of clarifying mandates, promoting coordination, conducting strategic planning, and ensuring available resources. In fact, a majority of local authorities cite the lack of or insufficient incentives (70%), financial (70%) and human resources (57%) as the main bottlenecks for the process to link citizens' development needs to the country's budget process more effectively. To that end, the OECD has identified several key recommendations to strengthen governance mechanisms, including:

- Clarifying the overall structure and organization of the needs assessment process;
- Ensuring greater multi-level coordination and transfer of information via the needs assessment process;
- Developing an effective strategic planning cycle in the needs assessment process;

- Strengthening the capacities and skills of public servants to conduct stakeholder participation activities in the needs assessment process; and
- Ensuring the continuity of participation initiatives through dedicated financial resources.

The role of public communication in supporting the needs assessment process at the sub-national level in Jordan

The needs assessment process would also benefit from improved communication around the decentralization reform, opportunities for participation and the results achieved. In fact, local authorities (63%) and civil society (57%) alike noted that low levels of awareness are one of the main challenges in promoting the participation of stakeholders. Sub-national authorities could thus focus on ensuring greater transparency and access to up-to-date, clear and relevant information, particularly on the criteria for selection of local projects as well as the final plan and budget. Beyond sharing information, local authorities should adopt a two-way communication approach, by tailoring their messaging and channels, as well as using interactive platforms – such as social media – to engage underrepresented segments of the population. To that end, the OECD has identified several key recommendations to strengthen the role of public communications in the needs assessment process, including:

- Establishing a more strategic communication approach for local governments;
- Strengthening implementation efforts around access to information (ATI) at the sub-national level;
- Promoting the proactive disclosure of relevant, clear and timely information on the process and results of collecting needs; and
- Developing a more sophisticated use of communication channels according to the needs and preferences of different audiences.

Stakeholder participation in the needs assessment process

Reaping the full benefits of decentralization will entail engaging stakeholders more meaningfully at all stages of the needs assessment process. Despite consultations taking place at the local and municipal level, opportunities remain to expand these initiatives across the subsequent phases of approving, implementing and evaluating local development plans. In addition, adopting different models of participation according to the needs of local communities – such as citizen panels, planning cells or town hall meetings – could promote meaningful avenues for engagement in local decision-making processes. While there is no one-size-fits-all model of stakeholder participation, the success of these initiatives will also depend on the existence of adequate legal and institutional mechanisms. To that end, the OECD has identified several key recommendations to strengthen the role of stakeholder participation in the needs assessment process, including:

- Promoting stakeholder participation throughout the needs assessment process;
- Enhancing opportunities for consultation and engagement at the local level; and
- Building mechanisms to support stakeholder participation at the local level

Assessment and Recommendations

The Decentralization Reform in Jordan

Key Economic, Social and Political factors shaping Decentralization in Jordan

The decentralization reform in Jordan can be better understood when assessed against a series of factors shaping its implementation – namely, economic, demographic, social and political.

Despite numerous reforms, Jordan is still facing a stagnant economy, growing income inequality levels and high unemployment rates. Income disparities not only highlight the timeliness and relevance of local development planning cycles to embed participation at its core, but to also ensure the integration of all regions and all citizens in economic and democratic life. With a highly young and dispersed population, the success of the decentralization reform will rely on the Government's ability to promote the participation of youth across the country in shaping local development policies. In response to deteriorating trust levels and growing perceptions of corruption, the Government would also benefit from continuing efforts to strengthen integrity systems within subnational institutions, as part of existing efforts in the framework of the National Integrity Charter and its Executive Plan. Broadly, the implementation of decentralization and open government reforms at the local level must respond to an evolving political and governance landscape in Jordan, as it transitions from a highly centralized to a progressively deconcentrated system with more powers vested at the Governorate and Municipal level.

The recent Coronavirus (COVID-19) crisis has moreover highlighted the need for the central and local levels of government to act decisively, and in a coordinated manner, to respond to the both the public health and economic dimensions of the crisis.

The rollout of the Decentralization Reform in Jordan (2015 – 2020)

Over the last decade, Jordan has embarked on an ambitious reform path to promote good governance and strengthen democracy. The Decentralization (No. 49) and Municipalities (No. 41) Laws adopted in 2015 are an important reflection of the Government's commitment to place citizens at the heart of local policies and services. Notably, the laws introduced a new governance framework at the subnational level composed by elected and non-elected councils and a bottom-up approach for the design of local plans and budgets through a yearly collection and assessment of citizens' needs.

Since its adoption, the Government of Jordan has achieved important milestones in gradually decentralizing power to the local level. The establishment of the Inter-Ministerial Committee on Decentralization and the Executive Committee as oversight bodies were a key element to ensure the rollout of this reform. Following local elections in 2017, two rounds of the need collection cycle have ensued, providing valuable insights and lessons learned. Recognising the iterative nature of this reform, and responding to the concerns raised in the National Dialogues, a draft local administration law was presented to Parliament in early 2020. This new momentum for reform presents an opportunity to revamp the decentralization process by strengthening governance mechanisms, establishing a two-way dialogue with citizens and promoting opportunities for stakeholders to have a say in the decisions that affect their daily lives.

Main OECD survey findings

The OECD, together with MoPIC, conducted a survey in 2019 to understand the main gaps in the needs assessment and development planning process from the perspective of subnational authorities and civil society.

Findings from the survey conducted in coordination with sub-national authorities note a set of governance and stakeholder participation challenges emerging from the rollout of the decentralization reform (see Figure 1). On the one side, local governments have struggled to adapt to the profound and rapid reorganization of structures resulting from the 2015 laws. In fact, local authorities cited the lack of or insufficient incentives (70%), financial (70%) and human resources (57%) as the top three bottlenecks to the operational effectiveness of the needs assessment process. On the other side, the bottom-up process to design local development plans has drastically transformed the way in which sub-national authorities interact with citizens. Ensuring the meaningful involvement of stakeholders in this process has notably faced key barriers with high levels of distrust (65%) and low levels of awareness and capacity of stakeholders to participate (63%).

Figure 1. Main challenges of sub-national authorities to engage stakeholders in the needs assessment process

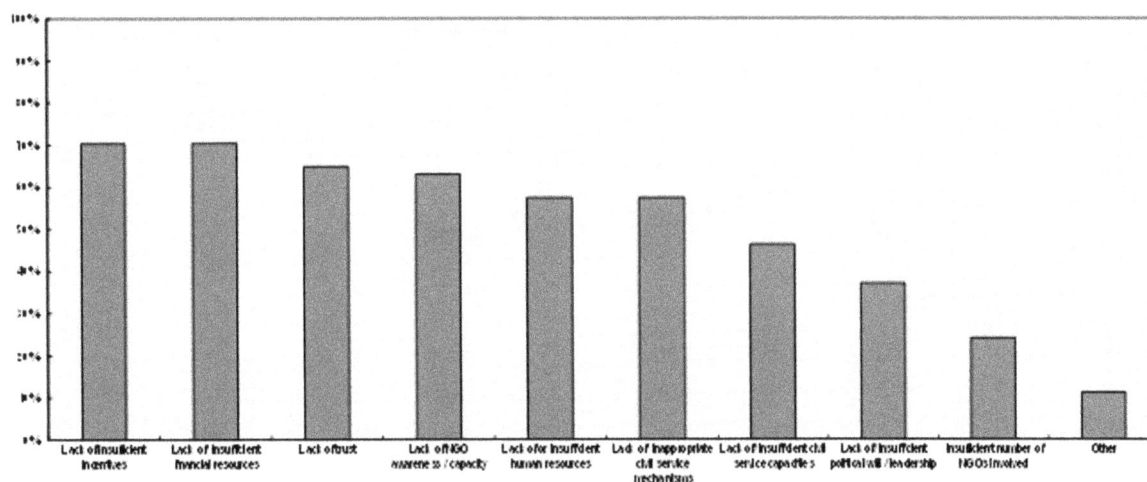

Source: OECD (2019) Questionnaire for sub-national governments: Stakeholder participation in Jordan's needs assessment process.

Most of these challenges were also highlighted by civil society (see Figure 2). Findings note that a majority of stakeholders consider the needs assessment to be a relevant process, but scepticism regarding its implementation yet remains. To illustrate, a majority of respondents noted the lack of trust (70%) and motivation (60%) as the main drivers of low participation. Beyond the willingness of citizens to engage, over half of respondents (57%) also attribute low degrees of engagement to the insufficient awareness raising of the benefits and available opportunities for participation.

Figure 2. Main challenges identified by civil society to engage stakeholders in the needs assessment process

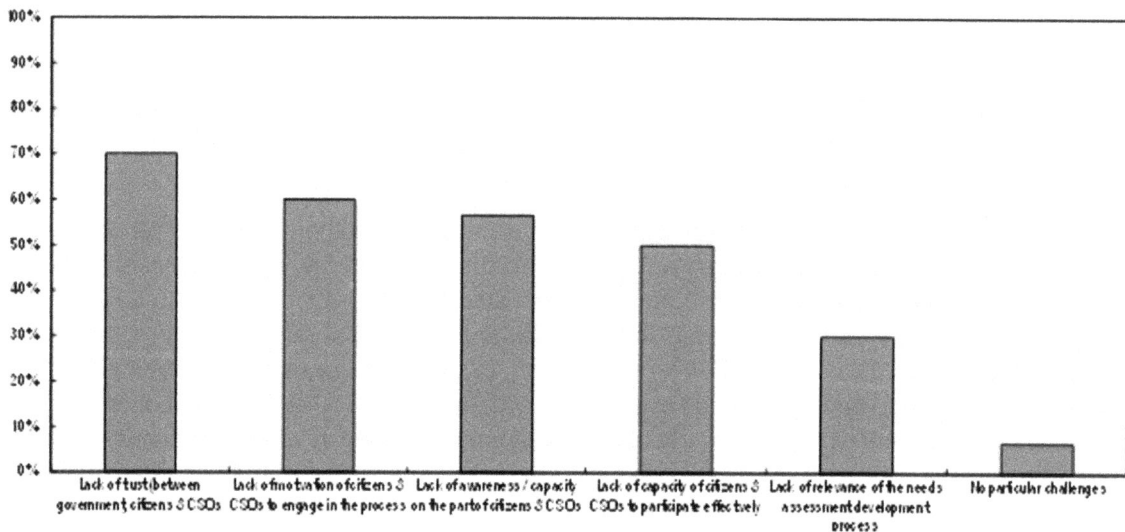

Source: OECD (2019), Questionnaire for Civil Society: Stakeholder participation in Jordan's needs assessment process.

Therefore, addressing existing gaps concerning both governance and stakeholder participation issues will serve as a basis to identify future avenues for support. There is a general acknowledgement of the benefits of decentralization, but there is yet road ahead to equip local governments for the successful deployment of the needs collection process. This report therefore takes stock of the progress achieved since the 2017 local elections, and identifies the challenges and opportunities ahead for sub-national governments.

Based on the extensive data collected, the OECD provides the Government of Jordan the following recommendations to mainstream the principles of transparency, integrity, accountability and stakeholder participation beyond the national level.

Good Governance Enablers in the Needs Assessment Process

The introduction of the 2015 Decentralization laws drastically transformed the structures, work and responsibilities of public institutions at the Governorate and Municipal level. The rapid speed and scale of this process, however, has exacerbated challenges in operationalizing new structures, consolidating formal procedures and meeting citizens growing expectations to participate in and contribute to local development policies. While the Government of Jordan has achieved great progress in implementing previous recommendations from the OECD (2017) report, findings reveal room for improvement to:

Clarifying the overall structure and organization of the Needs Assessment Process

Formal governance structures are key building blocks enabling actors, processes and outcomes to reach desired objectives. Acknowledging these benefits, the Government of Jordan has progressed in consolidating structures with the introduction of elected and non-elected councils at the Municipal and Governorate level. These structures in a majority of subnational entities (80%) have a dedicated person, unit or department in charge of stakeholder participation initiatives for the collection of needs.

Nevertheless, findings reveal a series of challenges to ensure the operational effectiveness of these structures. First, the exact roles and responsibilities between local, municipal and governorate actors are blurred, lack detailing and are not codified. Second, there is a need to clarify the relationship between members of Executive Councils and Governorate Councils for the development of local plans and budgets. Third, existing guidelines for the preparation of needs lists could be complemented with trainings and resources for stakeholders to carry out technical tasks in the context of the needs assessment process (i.e. consultations, cost benefit analysis and evaluation).

Ensuring greater multi-level coordination and transfer of information via the Needs Assessment process

As in most OECD countries, Jordan has developed formal and informal co-ordination mechanisms at the national level in the framework of the decentralization reform. Nonetheless, horizontal and vertical mechanisms have yet to be developed at the subnational level. The transversal nature of the needs assessment process offers new opportunities to solidify working relationships between local actors, establish formal procedures and align capabilities to share information. This will be particularly relevant to promote intra-governorate alignment on the work of elected and non-elected councils. To this end, the Government could consider the creation of informal thematic networks to align development projects, share lessons learned and promote the exchange of good practices.

Fostering an effective strategic planning cycle in the needs assessment process

Jordan has gradually established a robust multi-level strategic planning framework. At the national level, the Jordan 2025 Vision and the Renaissance Plan guide policy reform. A bottom-up approach to subnational planning was adopted with the Decentralization reform, where Governorate and Municipal needs manuals inform the design of each governorate strategy and executive plan. In 2020, the "Tanmiah Tool" was introduced to support the strategic management of the needs assessment process at the level of each governorate.

For the strategic planning process at the local level to reap its full benefits, the Government could transition from consulting on needs to co-creating plans with local stakeholders. This is all the more important, as OECD survey data revealed that close to a third of subnational governments consider that stakeholder contributions are not fully reflected in Governorate plans. Beyond the development of strategies, efforts could also focus on improving the link between local development projects, their financing, implementation and evaluation to inform subsequent planning cycles and better reflect local needs in national policies.

Strengthening the capacities and skills of public servants to conduct stakeholder participation activities in the needs assessment process

As the decentralization reform transforms the work of local authorities, it will be critical to ensure adequate levels of staffing and capabilities to engage stakeholders in local decision-making processes. In Jordan, a lack of human resources was selected as one of the top challenges in the needs-assessment process (57%), followed by bottle necks in terms of establishing necessary mechanisms (57%) and capacities (46%) within institutions. These findings align with those in regards to training, where despite their existence, public officials highlighted difficulties to carrying out technical tasks for the needs cycle. The Government of Jordan could thus focus on developing a more systemic approach to ensuring the coordination, relevance and sustainability of trainings reflecting on different skill levels across Governorates.

Ensuring the continuity of participation initiatives through dedicated financial resources

Adequate levels of financing within sub-national authorities are a sine qua non condition for the real decentralization of power to the local level, to support the increasing role of subnational entities in the delivery of many crucial services. As in many OECD countries, challenges in Jordan underline low levels of available funding for local development projects within governorates. OECD data revealed that in 2019 only 13% of respondents had a dedicated budget for the needs assessment process and only 2% for participation activities in general. Allocating dedicated funds would not only strengthen the capacity of GDUs and LDUs to engage with local communities, but would also incentivize the regularisation of stakeholder participation activities.

Recommendation	Key Activities	Responsibilities	Outputs
Clarifying the overall structure and organization of the Needs Assessment Process	• Map the needs assessment process and codify the specific roles and responsibilities of each stakeholder involved.	MoLA and MoI	• Codified roles and responsibilities for local, municipal, and governorate authorities. • Guidelines developed for implementing and monitoring local development plans. • Trainings conducted for stakeholders in project management and M&E.
	• Differentiate tasks of stakeholders in Municipal, Executive and Governorate Councils, as well as for LDUs and GDUs.	MoLA and MoI	
	• Clarify functions and sub-tasks regarding the four main stages of the needs assessment process, namely planning, budgeting, implementing, and evaluating for each level of government.	MoLA and MoI	
	• Disseminate relevant information to stakeholders in each of the 12 governorates through the creation of a centralized information repository where all guidelines, training calendars, and other relevant information can be found.	MoLA and MoI	
	• Include concrete procedures and instructions in existing guidelines for local development units to standardize activities throughout municipalities and governorates, such as required quarterly hearings or annual evaluation reports.	MoLA and MoI	
Ensuring greater multi-level coordination and transfer of information via the Needs Assessment process	• Establish procedural requirements to foster multi-level coordination, including mandating local, municipal and governorate councils to make publicly available their needs list documents as well as publishing a follow-up report on the needs assessment, budget allocations, and the status of implementation of local projects.	MoLA and MoI	• Publication of needs lists and monitoring reports. • Informal thematic working groups created • Periodic meetings of local, municipal and governorate officials.
	• Include representatives from Local and Municipal Councils in regular meetings between the Governorate and Executive Councils.	Governorate Councils	
	• Establish formal sub-national co-ordination mechanisms, such as a yearly forum between local authorities or thematic communities of practice, in order to share experiences, lessons learnt and to identify common challenges and opportunities in pushing the decentralization agenda forward.	MoLA. MoI and MoPIC	

Objective	Actions	Responsible	Outputs
Fostering an effective strategic planning cycle in the Needs Assessment process	• Ensure the reflection of local needs into governorate and national development plans in order to strengthen the technical capacity of GDUs and LDUs to support the participatory nature of the process.	Governorate councils in coordination with MoPIC, MoI and MoLA	• Trainings conducted for GDUs and LGUs. • Adoption of the Adat Altanmyah tool. • Adoption of the Tanmiah System across local, municipal and governorate entities
	• Strengthen the link between the development of plans, their financing and their implementation. The government could also consider formalizing or regularizing the evaluation of plans to support this process further.	MoPIC	
	• Support the transformation of the strategic planning process at the sub-national level from the collection of wish lists to the creation of a more structured approach through innovative forms of stakeholder participation that promote co-creation.	MoPIC. MoLA and MoI	
Strengthening the capacities and skills of public servants to conduct stakeholder participation activities in the needs assessment process	• Map skills gaps across the 12 governorates in order to better adapt trainings to the needs of local governments.	MoLA and MoI	• Trainings conducted for stakeholders in project M&E, needs assessment processes, and consultations. • Catalogue and/or online repository of training materials developed.
	• Design and implement a series of technical training modules to ensure the necessary capacities and skills at the governorate and municipal levels exist to carry out the needs assessment process.	MoLA and MoI	
	• Provide technical and specialized trainings to GDUs and LDUs, in particular on how to carry out stakeholder participation related initiatives in the context of the needs assessment process. Trainings could also focus on building and managing a number of transparency and accountability tools, such as open data portals, citizen budgets, community planning and participatory budgeting.	MoLA and MoI	
	• Explore potential partnerships with other stakeholders, such as NGOs and donors, who also provide trainings related to participation at the local level in order to create synergies, including with the Institute of Public Administration.	MoLA and MoI	
	• Develop a catalogue of existing trainings and disseminate it across the 12 governorates in close coordination with NGOs.	MoLA and MoI	
Ensuring the continuity of participation initiatives through dedicated financial resources	• Map the present and future financing needs to set realistic budget limits for each governorate based on available funding, national and regional priorities, local needs, and results from previous budgetary allocations.	MoLA and MoI	• Development of medium-term resource cash flow assessments at sub-national level. • Established dedicated budget lines for conducting Needs Assessment activities.
	• Allocate and standardize a dedicated budget line in each governorate to carry out participation activities, both in the framework of the needs assessment process and beyond.	MoF	
	• Map the existing pool of external sources of funding that could be leveraged to fund opportunities to engage with stakeholders, build capacity to carry out these activities, ensure sectorial studies match with the proposed needs/projects, etc.	MoLA, MoI, MoPIC and MoF	

The role of public communication in supporting the needs assessment process at the subnational level in Jordan

Public communication can bridge the divide between subnational governments and citizens by transforming the way in which these actors interact in the design of local development plans and budgets. Beyond simply serving to disseminate information, this function can help establish a two-way dialogue with the public, raise awareness around key reforms, change behaviours and impact the policy making process.

The Government of Jordan could consider the following analysis to leverage the contribution of public communication to promote the principles of transparency, integrity, accountability and stakeholder participation across the needs assessment process:

Establishing a more strategic communication approach for local governments

In Jordan, subnational administrations interact regularly with citizens as part of the process to collect needs, but evidence revealed that public communication is carried out on an ad hoc and informal basis. For instance, public communication plans in 69% of Municipal and Governorate entities are not in written form, formalized or widely distributed. A focus on strengthening communication structures, modernizing communication capacities and addressing uneven levels of skills will be critical to support a more strategic communication approach between government and citizens. Indeed, coordinating communication initiatives across and within Governorates could also help local authorities speak with one voice to avoid contradictory messaging and promote internal information sharing.

Strengthening implementation efforts around the Access to Information (ATI) right at the subnational level

While Jordan was the first country in the MENA region to adopt an ATI law in 2007, efforts could be expanded at the local level to equip institutions with the necessary knowledge, tools and skills to proactively share information on the needs cycle and more broadly. On the one side, findings suggest that information on final local development plans, lists of approved needs or calendars of participation initiatives could be made available in an easy, clear and understandable format for the public. On the other, the effective implementation of this right will also require formalising procedures for Municipal and Governorate entities to respond to information requests and prove technical assistance for their effective deployment. There is an opportunity at present to solidify the country's strong commitment to guaranteeing this right by targeting local actors within commitments in future Open Government Partnership (OGP) national action plans (NAPs).

Promoting the proactive disclosure of relevant, clear and timely information on the process and results of collecting needs

For the needs assessment process to successfully integrate citizens in the local development planning process, the Government could leverage public communication as a tool to promote transparency and raise awareness around key activities, procedures and results. This is all the more important, as OECD data revealed that two thirds of local authorities attribute low levels of participation in the needs cycle to the lack of awareness of stakeholders around this process. This finding aligns with those from OECD survey results showing that a large share of civil society was not aware of the criteria used to define priorities for local investments (77%), results communicated (83%) or needs funded in the plan (90%). To this end, providing timely, relevant and accessible information in this regard can help combat feelings of scepticism around the decentralization reform and in turn support the ability of stakeholders to meaningfully contribute to local development plans.

Developing a more sophisticated use of communication channels according to the needs and preferences of different audiences

Establishing a two-way communication approach requires governments to understand the needs, perceptions, fears and habits of different audiences to deliver more effective messages. At present, subnational authorities and the public generally agree that social media platforms, formal letters, emails and phone calls are the best means to communicate on the needs assessment process. Nonetheless, for these channels to achieve their desired objectives, local authorities should progressively aim at tailoring messages to different age, demographic and interest groups. The selection of channels should also consider the needs and habits of different audiences, such as those from vulnerable segments of the population in Jordan who may not have internet access or may have low levels of digital literacy.

There is an opportunity at present to leverage the interactivity benefits of social media platforms to engage stakeholders across the needs assessment process, given its popular use by local authorities (72%) and citizens (73%). With a large share of the population aged below 30, subnational governments could open dedicated spaces for the online participation of youth to promote their inclusion in the design of local policies. Nonetheless, to reap their full benefits, a set of social media guidelines could be developed to promote a more strategic use of these platforms.

Recommendation	Key Activities	Responsibilities	Outputs
Establishing a more strategic communications approach for local governments	• Develop a written communication plan based on audience insights to institutionalize communication activities, build awareness and buy-in efforts within government, and support the monitoring and evaluation of communication activities.	Governorate and Local Councils	• Development of written communications plan for Needs Assessments activities
	• Develop a national communications strategy for the decentralization process, to clarify how to inform citizens of the available opportunities for participation, the overall process of the needs assessment, its progress and impact achieved.	MoLA, MoI and MoSMA	• Develop a national communications strategy for the decentralization process
	• Build the capacities of local civil servants to ensure they have the skills to communicate effectively with stakeholders throughout the phases of the needs assessment process (i.e. data analytics, social media use and online participation methods, etc.).	MoLA, MoI and MoSMA	• Trainings conducted to modernized communications capabilities
	• Develop a communication manual or a set of guidelines to help standardize procedures, clarify roles, and promote a more coordinated approach between the three levels of government.	MoLA, MoI and MoSMA	• Adopt tools for improved coordination.
	• Coordinate messages and communication activities between local and governorate levels using new digital platforms – such as Trello, Slack and WhatsApp – to facilitate internal communication between government stakeholders from local, municipal and governorate levels.	LDUs and GDUs	
	• Improve the coordination of actors and public communication activities at the local level.	Local Development Councils	

Strengthening implementation efforts around the Access to Information (ATI) right at the subnational level	• Clarify the rules and procedures around how public institutions categorize and share information, as well as the information flows with citizens.	Open Government Unit in MoPIC and National Library	• Development of a one-stop-shop/portal for information sharing
	• Promote the proactive disclosure the needs assessment results and the approved list through coordination with the National Library to increase the quality and frequency of data shared with the public.		
	• Consider expanding the scope of existing ATI commitments in the country's open government agenda to explicitly target local actors.		• Adoption of implementation protocols to respond to ATI requests.
Promoting the proactive disclosure of relevant, clear and timely information on the process and results of collecting needs	• Clarify and publish the criteria for selection of budget priorities from the early stages of the needs cycle.	Governorate Councils	• Publication of section criteria for budgeting and results of final/approved LDPs and budgets.
	• Facilitate the process of communicating results and impact to citizens, which in turn could help raise awareness and buy-in regarding the decentralization process.	Governorate Councils	
Developing a more sophisticated use of communication channels according to the needs and preferences of different audiences	• Map audiences and employ a diverse range of communication channels to reach a variety of stakeholders to reflect different needs and media consumption patterns.	Subnational authorities, GDUs and LDUs	• Development on online spaces for participation.
	• Use social media to communicate with citizens, including social media guidelines, capacity building of public communicators, and the development of new and relevant skills to match users' needs.	Sub-national authorities as well as MoLA/MoSMA/MoI.	• Development of social media guidelines.
	• Develop a specific engagement plan tailored to the needs of different segments of the population, based on demographic factors and regional needs, including sharing information with vulnerable segments of the population.	Sub-national authorities as well as MoLA/MoSMA/MoI	• Development of tailored communications products and trainings.
	• Develop a specific engagement plan with youth, making use of social media platforms, to increase their participation in the design and delivery of local development plans.	Sub-national authorities as well as MoLA/MoSMA/MoI	

Stakeholder Participation in the Needs Assessment Process

Following the adoption of the Decentralization laws and the establishment of elected and non-elected councils, the Government of Jordan has achieved key milestones in placing citizens at the heart of the local development planning process. Notably, the Government reinstated its commitment to prioritizing stakeholder participation at the subnational level, acknowledging it as an important pillar of its national vision – the Renaissance Plan (2019 – 2020). Moreover, it consolidated efforts to engage local communities as part of this reform with dedicated commitments in the country's 3rd and 4th OGP NAPs. Engagement around political reform for decentralization has also advanced in the framework of the country's National Dialogues.

Despite the progress achieved in terms of opening the decision making process for local development plans, there is room to leverage participation to better inform, consult and engage stakeholders. To this end, the Government of Jordan could consider:

Promoting stakeholder participation throughout the needs assessment process

The cyclic nature of needs assessment process in Jordan represents an opportunity for subnational authorities to integrate a wide diversity of stakeholders in the design of local policies and services. To ensure that outcomes respond to citizens' expectations, participation could be further mainstreamed throughout all phases of identifying local needs, drafting governorate plans, implementing development initiatives and their evaluation. At present, OECD evidence revealed varying degrees of participation across this process, where most initiatives focus on the collection of needs but diminish in the validation and approval stages of local development plans. Ensuring the co-creation of plans with stakeholders could help secure buy-in, as OECD data suggests that only 20% of civil society felt contributions were reflected in final plans and 53% considered that this was unclear.

Enhancing opportunities for consultation and engagement at the local level

To mainstream participation in the needs assessment process, the Government of Jordan could transition from consulting needs toward establishing a co-creation process for local development plans and budgets. While the consolidation of participation activities by LDUs has advance following the 2017 local elections, these are conducted on an ad hoc basis and their representativeness vary across large and small governorates. In fact, OECD data found that less than half of responding civil society stakeholders have participated in the needs assessment process. To counter disengagement in public life, OECD evidence suggests that efforts could focus on addressing existing challenges hindering the involvement of stakeholders, including the lack of trust, lack of awareness and lack of communication around the decentralization reform.

Building mechanisms to support stakeholder participation at the local level

The creation of new participation opportunities in the needs assessment process alone, however, will not ensure the relevance and legitimacy of local development plans. For their successful implementation, the Government of Jordan could consider the development of mechanisms in the form of standards, guidelines and formal procedures for local, municipal and governorate actors. Moreover, efforts will also be needed to ensure the ability of citizens, civil society and businesses to participate in the development of local development plans. With the advent of the new draft local administration law, there is also an opportunity to consolidate an enabling environment for stakeholder participation activities through their acknowledgments and formalisation therein. This would also be an important step toward establishing a culture of openness and continuous learning, as has been done through existing platforms such as the National Dialogue.

Recommendation	Key Activities	Responsibilities	Outputs
Promoting stakeholder participation throughout the Needs Assessment process	• Increase the scope of activities for citizens to participate throughout all the stages of the needs assessment process, in particular at the drafting and validating phases of local development plans.	LDUs and GDUs	• Development of participation opportunities for the drafting and validation of LDPs.

Enhancing opportunities for consultation and engagement at the local level.	• Consider the development of participatory commitments in selected governorates, which can be included in the next OGP action plan.	MoPIC Open Government Unit	• Consolidation of consultations with municipal and governorate public officials. • Adoption of mechanism to monitor participation. • Inclusion of participatory processes in selected/pilot governorates. • Development and dissemination of consultation guidelines.
	• Building on the experience of Salt, consider expanding its current OGP collaboration to engage several municipalities in the OGP Local Programme.	MoPIC Open Government Unit	
	• Coordinate joint consultations with citizens and municipalities on the transferred document of needs, for example, to increase ownership and buy-in.	LDUs and GDUs	
	• Assign clear institutional responsibilities for stakeholder participation for local, municipal and governorate actors, including LDUs and GDUs.	MoI, MoLA, and MoPIC	
	• Develop and adopt a mechanism for governorate and municipal entities to document the levels of participation in local activities.	MoI, MoLA, and MoPIC	
	• Consider adopting engagement practices such as citizen panels, planning cells and other deliberative processes.	Local, Municipal and Governorate authorities collecting needs	
	• Consider the inclusion of provisions to institutionalise consultations and other participation related initiatives as part of the ongoing reform of the Local Administration Law.	MoLA and MoI	
	• Develop a set of consultation guidelines aimed at all government stakeholders focused on: (i) How to engage stakeholders at each stage of the needs assessment process and map processes and opportunities for participation; (ii) How to ensure representativeness and diversity of stakeholders and establish criteria to identify stakeholders; (iii) How to validate inputs by citizens; and (iv) How to communicate throughout the process and about results to maximize impact.	MoPIC open government unit together with MoLA and MoI	
Building mechanisms to support stakeholder participation at the local level	• Develop a set of criteria or standards on how citizens can develop their list of needs, which can be included in the manual shared with municipal stakeholders by national authorities.	MoPIC open government unit together with MoLA and MoI	• Development of standards guidelines, and procedures. • Outreach activities conducting to improve the awareness of CSOs on the means available to contribute to the process.
	• Design and carry out more capacity building modules aimed at providing civil society organizations with the appropriate tools, guidelines and skills to leverage their important role throughout the process.	MoLA and MoI	
	• Expand on the National Dialogue to develop a formal multi-stakeholder platform to promote an open dialogue between government representatives, civil society, private sector and citizens from different local communities. The platform could take the form of an innovation lab or an informal network of mayors to share best practices, reflect on lessons learned, identify common challenges and solutions to promote stakeholder participation	MoLA and MoI	

Chapter 1.

Decentralization in Jordan: Context and background

This chapter will reflect on the conditions under which Jordan's decentralization reform efforts arose, the issues shaping its pace and scale, and its potential to support the further opening of the government. It will do so by outlining the role of open government as an instrument to streamline the principles of transparency, integrity, accountability and stakeholder participation at the local level in the country. The chapter will also explore the contextual factors influencing the implementation of decentralization in Jordan, as well as its main tenants and progress achieved to date. It will conclude with an outline of the methodology of this report.

Introduction

With the passing in 2015 of the Decentralization and Municipality laws, the Government of Jordan acted on its intention to bring decision-making closer to citizens and to increase their engagement in directing and planning policy interventions. Broadly, the aim of such efforts is "to transfer a range of powers, responsibilities and resources from central to sub-national authorities" (OECD, 2019a) and to bring governments closer to citizens. Beyond regulatory implications, furthermore, these reforms have wide-ranging effects on economic development, governance and the relationship between politicians, civil servants and the public at large.

As highlighted in the OECD's 2017 Jordan report *Towards a New Partnership with Citizens*, decentralization reforms across and beyond OECD countries vary significantly in their scope and degree (See Box 1.1 on different theoretical approaches to decentralization). The implementation of these type of reforms, furthermore, may differ from sweeping to incremental, and may cover political, administrative and fiscal dimensions (OECD, 2019a).

Box 1.1. Theoretical approaches to decentralisation

Decentralisation: the transfer of responsibility to democratically independent lower levels of government, thereby giving them more managerial discretion, but not necessarily more financial independence.

It usually includes:

- *Political* decentralisation refers to a situation in which political power is moved either to regional or local bodies that are elected, or to administrative actors who are appointed and supervised by elected bodies. Political decentralisation requires effective constitutional, legal, and regulatory frameworks to ensure accountability and transparency.

- Fiscal decentralisation is the most comprehensive form of decentralisation as it is directly linked to budgetary practices. It involves resource reallocation to sub-national authorities. Fiscal decentralisation touches upon all forms of decentralisation; reallocating responsibilities without assigning sufficient levels of resources to the newly empowered units will not result in effective decentralisation.

- Administrative *decentralisation* aims to transfer the position of the decision-making authority and responsibility for the delivery of select public services from the central government to other levels of government or agencies. Some of its variants include:

  a. *Delegation* assigns – usually by administrative decree – decision-making authority for specifically defined functions to local units of government or agencies that are not necessarily branches or local offices of the decentralising authority. In terms of education decentralisation, responsibility is transferred to elected or appointed education governance bodies, such as school councils or school management.

  b. *Deconcentration* transfers decision-making authority – often by administrative decree – from a higher to a lower level of bureaucracy within the same level of government. The same hierarchical accountability is maintained between local units and the central government ministry or agency that has been decentralised. Deconcentration is often the first step undertaken by newly decentralised governments to improve service delivery, that is, the transfer of responsibility from central ministries to field offices or more autonomous agencies, thereby becoming closer to citizens while remaining part of central government.

  c. *Devolution* is the moving of political power from the top to the bottom. It involves a permanent – legal or constitutional – transfer of responsibility, decision making, resources and revenues from a higher level of government to a lower, local level that enjoys substantial autonomy from the decentralising authority. In terms of education decentralisation, devolution transfers responsibility for education to lower levels of government, such as governorates, municipalities, or districts.

Source: OECD (2017a), *Towards a New Partnership with Citizens: Jordan's Decentralisation Reform*, OECD Public Governance Reviews, OECD Publishing, Paris, https://doi.org/10.1787/9789264275461-en.

It is therefore important to acknowledge that there is not a one-size-fits all approach for decentralization, but rather its execution should be seen as a dynamic and continuous process. Indeed, the deployment of these reforms does not follow a linear trajectory, as it responds to shifting economic, social, and institutional factors. Acknowledging these complexities is important since decentralization reforms can so clearly serve as a means to achieve medium and long-term policy goals, such as enabling more efficient service delivery, advancing democratic reforms and promoting economic development (OECD, 2019a). This is especially true in light of the ongoing Coronavirus (COVID-19) pandemic, as the crisis response will need to occur at both the central and local levels to ensure continued delivery of vital health services as well as measures to support vulnerable groups and the private sector.

Recognizing this potential, the Government of Jordan has embarked on an ambitious process to decentralize power from the central to the sub-national level. Notably, in 2014, His Majesty King Abdullah II emphasized that "political development should start at the grassroots level, and then move up to decision making centres and not vice versa" (OECD, 2017a). Therefore, one of the most important objectives of the decentralization reform, later reinforced by Jordan's 2025 vision[1], is to place citizens at the heart of policies and services by granting local authorities a major role in their co-design and co-delivery.

While much has been achieved with the 2017 local elections and two rounds of the needs assessment cycle, the promise of decentralization in Jordan has yet to fully meet citizens' growing expectations. This chapter will therefore explore the conditions under which decentralization arose in Jordan, the possible implications shaping its pace and scale, as well as the potential of this reform to support the further opening of the government. The first section will outline the role of open government as an instrument to embed the principles of transparency, integrity accountability and stakeholder participation across levels of government. The chapter will then proceed to outline the economic, demographic, social and political factors that have shaped the decentralization process in Jordan. It will end by outlining the main tenants of the reform, its current progress, as well as the methodology of this report.

Open Government as a key lever supporting decentralization in Jordan

Open government reforms are built on the idea that promoting transparency, integrity, accountability and stakeholder participation enables governments to work better, deliver the services their constituencies need, and ultimately enhance trust in the legitimacy of decisions. Given these benefits, the OECD defines open government as "a culture of governance that promotes the principles of transparency, integrity, accountability and stakeholder participation in support of democracy and inclusive growth" (OECD, 2017b).

With the growing adoption of open government reforms, countries are increasingly mainstreaming these principles across sub-national levels. Local governments (i.e. regional, provincial and municipal) can have a close and direct impact on people's daily lives. Not only are local governments often responsible for the delivery of crucial services, but they also play an intermediary role between the public and national administrations. Furthermore, sub-national governments are often more present, and have a better understanding of public priorities as well as differences in needs. Implementing reforms at the local level may therefore offer the greatest opportunity to transform the relationship between the government and its citizens through meaningful and direct opportunities for participation in public life.

Against this backdrop, the OECD Recommendation of the Council on Open Government recognizes the roles and prerogatives of local governments under the concept of an Open State (See Box 1.2). Under provision 10, the Recommendation argues for the streamlining of open government strategies and initiatives across levels of government and branches of power. While this concept emphasises improving the quality and consistency of governance throughout a country, it also highlights the importance of collaborating, exploiting synergies, and sharing good practices and lessons learned with stakeholders to promote open government principles. Broadly, this provision reflects the growing demands of citizens to take part in local decision-making.

Box 1.2. The OECD Recommendation of the Council on Open Government

The OECD Recommendation of the Council on Open Government is the first international legal instrument outlining 10 provisions for the implementation of successful open government strategies and initiatives:

1. Take measures in all branches and at all levels of the government to develop and implement open government strategies and initiatives in collaboration with stakeholders, and to foster commitment from politicians, members of parliaments, senior public managers and public officials, to ensure successful implementation and to prevent or overcome obstacles related to resistance to change.

2. Ensure the existence and implementation of the necessary open government legal and regulatory framework, including through the provision of supporting documents such as guidelines and manuals, while establishing adequate oversight mechanisms to ensure compliance.

3. Ensure the successful operationalisation and take-up of open government strategies and initiatives by: (i) providing public officials with the mandate to design and implement successful open government strategies and initiatives, as well as the adequate human, financial and technical resources, while promoting a supportive organisational culture (ii) promoting open government literacy in the administration, at all levels of government, and among stakeholders.

4. Co-ordinate, through the necessary institutional mechanisms, open government strategies and initiatives – horizontally and vertically – across all levels of government to ensure that they are aligned with and contribute to all relevant socio-economic objectives.

5. Develop and implement monitoring, evaluation and learning mechanisms for open government strategies and initiatives by: (i) identifying institutional actors to be in charge of collecting and disseminating up-to-date and reliable information and data in an open format (ii) developing comparable indicators to measure processes, outputs, outcomes and impact in collaboration with stakeholders (iii) fostering a culture of monitoring, evaluation and learning among public officials by increasing their capacity to regularly conduct exercises for these purposes in collaboration with relevant stakeholders.

6. Actively communicate on open government strategies and initiatives, as well as on their outputs, outcomes and impacts, in order to ensure that they are well known within and outside government, to favour their uptake and to stimulate stakeholder buy-in.

7. Proactively make available clear, complete, timely, reliable and relevant public sector data and information that is free of cost, available in an open and non-proprietary machine-readable format, easy to find, understand, use and reuse, and disseminated through a multi-channel approach, to be prioritised in consultation with stakeholders.

8. Grant all stakeholders equal and fair opportunities to be informed and consulted and actively engage them in all phases of the policy cycle, service design and delivery. This should be done with adequate time and at minimal cost, while avoiding duplication to minimise consultation fatigue. Further, specific efforts should be dedicated to reaching out to the most relevant, vulnerable, underrepresented or marginalised groups in society, while avoiding undue influence and policy capture.

9. Promote innovative ways to effectively engage with stakeholders to source ideas and co-create solutions, and seize the opportunities provided by digital government tools, including through the use of open government data, to support the achievement of the objectives of open government strategies and initiatives.

> 10. While recognising the roles, prerogatives and overall independence of all concerned parties, and according to their existing legal and institutional frameworks, explore the potential of moving from the concept of open government toward that of the open state.
>
> Source: OECD (2017b), Recommendation of the Council on Open Government, OECD, Paris, https://legalinstruments.oecd.org/en/instruments/OECD-LEGAL-0438.

Despite the recognized importance of the role of sub-national authorities in supporting open government principles, challenges remain to effectively mainstream an overarching open government agenda across and beyond levels of government. Notably, the OECD has identified a number of challenges specific to the local level, including:

- Limited awareness of the benefits of open government;
- Insufficient involvement of sub-national levels in national decision making processes;
- Limited human and financial resources as well as competing priorities (OECD, 2016).

For its part, Jordan has taken important steps to promote a culture of open government. Jordan was the first country in the MENA region to pass an Access to Information (ATI) law in 2007 and to join the Open Government Partnership (OGP) in 2011. In 2019, the country conducted the most inclusive process to design its fourth OGP action plan and is promoting the implementation needs of all commitments therein.

The ongoing decentralization process in Jordan thus represents an opportunity to consolidate these gains at the sub-national level. The bottom-up approach to the development of local development plans through decentralization brings new opportunities to involve citizens in more direct and meaningful ways. However, to reap these potential gains, there is a clear need to streamline and institutionalize practices to promote a more transparent, accountable and participatory needs assessment process across the 12 Governorates.

The Political Landscape in Jordan

The implementation of decentralization and open government reforms at the local level must adapt to the evolving political and governance landscape in Jordan. This is ever more true given the asymmetric challenges posed by the Coronavirus (COVID-19) pandemic, which demands a proactive and coordinated policy response to support the delivery of vital services and the rebuilding of economic livelihoods at both the central and local levels.

Jordan is a constitutional monarchy operating under a parliamentary system. His Royal Highness King Abdullah II retains authority over the country's overall strategic direction and the appointment of the government (i.e. prime minister, heads of ministries, governors, etc.). Following the Arab Spring, a series of reforms opened this system, including the appointment of the prime minister and government, which now occurs in consultation with parliament (Economist Intelligence Unit, 2019).

Jordan is transitioning from a highly centralized to a progressively deconcentrated system with more powers vested at the Governorate and Municipal level. The multi-level governance system in the country divides the Kingdom in 12 Governorates comprised of 100 Municipalities. Each Governorate is headed by a Governor appointed by the King, who responds directly to the Ministry of Interior (MoI) regarding the execution of national policies (Ranko Et Al, 2017). Supporting its work, Executive Councils are tasked with developing the Governorate's budget and executive plan, which is subsequently discussed and approved by the elected members of the Governorate Council. Although the political structures within municipalities vary significantly due to considerable differences in size, roles include a mayor, a municipal council as well as a local council. The new 2020 Municipalities law mandates the Ministry of Local Affairs (MoLA) to support and steer the work of municipalities on identifying needs from local communities. However, difficulties to bridge the divide between the operational effectiveness of these entities and the delivery of services coexists with the need to make national policies more relevant for the local level.

Contextualizing Decentralization – Key Economic, Social and Political factors shaping the Jordanian approach

Jordan's decentralization reforms are taking place within – and in response to – challenging national circumstances. Stagnating economic growth, growing perceptions of corruption, large influxes of refugees, and the evolving political landscape have affected the trajectory of this reform and have helped push the government to engage more fully with citizens' needs and expectations. Likewise, the recent Coronavirus (COVID-19) crisis has highlighted the need for the central and local levels of government to act decisively, and in a coordinated manner, to respond to the both the public health and economic dimensions of the crisis. This section therefore explores the elements influencing decentralization in Jordan, and analyses the ongoing challenges as well as the opportunities for open government to be at the centre of this paradigm shift.

Addressing stagnant economic growth, high-income disparities and unemployment across Jordan

Despite numerous reforms, Jordan faces a number of internal and external pressures that have slowed its progress in regards to economic development. In 2019, the rate of economic growth slowed significantly from an expected rate of 5% to 2.2% in real terms (Kardoosh, 2019). Stagnant economic growth in the country can be linked to mounting regional pressures, most visibly the crisis in Syria and, prior to that, Iraq, which have caused influxes of refugees that have strained health and education services and disrupted trade routes (World Bank, 2019). In fact, overall economic growth in the MENA region has also slowed, with growth forecasts expected to range from 1.5% to 3.5% from 2019 to 2021. This slowdown may be further exacerbated by the Coronavirus (COVID-19) pandemic, which has substantially weakened Jordan's near-term growth prospects (World Bank, 2020a).

The slow and unequal distribution of economic benefits across society in Jordan has in turn increased pressures for the government to deliver broad-based results. Around 15.7% of the population in the country live in extreme poverty[2], and these rates display significant variances across Governorates (Jordan Department of Statistics, 2019; Middle East Monitor, 2019). In the context of the Coronavirus (COVID-19) pandemic, the World Bank (2020) notes that Jordanian households are feeling the impact of this economic shock mainly through job losses and reduced earnings, and near poor households risk being pushed into poverty (World Bank, 2020a). To be sure, recent estimates suggests that poverty rates may increase by up to 21.6% as additional households are pushed over the poverty line (defined as $1.90 / day in 2011 PPP) (World Bank, 2020b).

From a socio-economic perspective, income disparities persist across Governorates and between urban and rural communities. According to the Kingdom of Jordan's Department of Statistics (2019), Amman is home to over 40% of the total population, and more than half of all households in the country (59%) in 2018 fell into high or upper middle-income segments. Indeed, wealth distribution varies significantly by region, with the North having the highest number of low-income households (29%) compared to the Central (15%) and Southern (23%) regions. Government data also found that a majority of the population in Madaba (61%), Mafraq (75%), Jarash (59%), Ajloun (55%), Tafiela (57%), and Ma'an (60%) fall in the lowest income quantiles (See Figure 1.1). Such disparities highlight the need to engage with a wider variety of local stakeholders, including traditionally underrepresented segments of the population from less profitable regions, to ensure local development policies address differing needs in the country.

Figure 1.1. Household wealth by residence in Jordan (2017-2018)

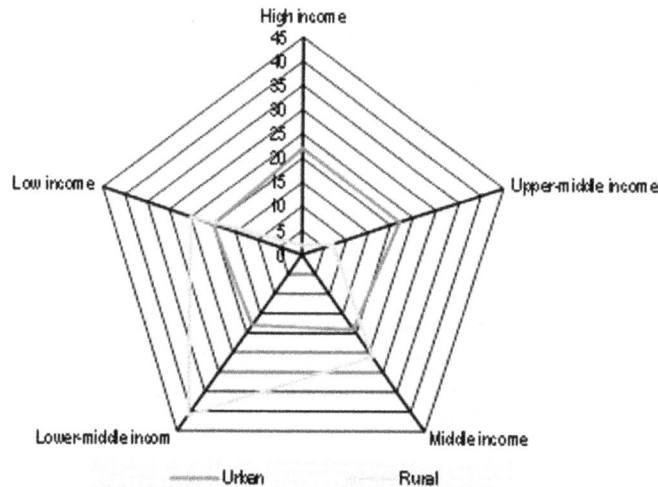

Note: Percent distribution of de jure population by wealth quintiles.
Source: The Kingdom of Jordan's Department of Statistics (2019) Jordan Population and Family Health Survey 2017-18, https://www.dhsprogram.com/pubs/pdf/FR346/FR346.pdf

Jordan's challenging economic situation is also reflected in its growing unemployment rates. Unemployment in Jordan is at a record high, increasing from an average rate of 14.12% to 19% from 2015 until 2019 (Jordan Department of Statistics, 2019; Jordan Times, 2019). The study published by the Kingdom of Jordan's Department of Statistics also identified geographic disparities in unemployment rates, with the highest levels (21.7%) in Zarqa, compared to the lowest levels (14.4%) in Karak. In addition to geographic variances, unemployment patterns showed a consistent gender divide, with unemployment among males reaching 16.4% in comparison to 28.9% for women. This situation risks generating, on the one side, a general sense of discontentment towards institutions and, on the other side, mounting expectations regarding the government's commitment to empower local communities through decentralization.

Acknowledging these challenges, the Government of Jordan is pursuing a series of structural economic reforms. The current administration developed a comprehensive *Economic Stimulus Growth Plan* (2018 – 2022) with the aim to "restore the momentum of economic growth and exploit the potential for development in Jordan". The plan introduces a series of economic, fiscal and sectoral strategies to improve the overall business environment and reach a target growth rate of 5% by 2022. New regulation was also enacted to achieve these ambitious goals, particularly in regards to financial transactions and public procurement systems. These efforts have positioned Jordan as one of the top 20 performers in the 2019 *Doing Business Index* (World Bank, 2019).

Nevertheless, Jordanians remain generally dissatisfied with the performance and opportunities for socio-economic development in the country. A majority of the population (71%) consider the current state of the economy as the biggest challenge facing Jordan, followed by corruption (17%) and the quality of public services (4%) (Arab Barometer, 2019) (See Figure 1.2). Perceptions of economic conditions have also declined, with 23% of the population rating the economy as favourable, in contrast with 46% in 2016 (Arab Barometer, 2019). Through consultation and engagement, open government initiatives can serve as a tool for Governorates to better reflect the needs of citizens and ensure their integration into the labour force.

Figure 1.2. Most important challenges facing Jordan from the perspective of citizens

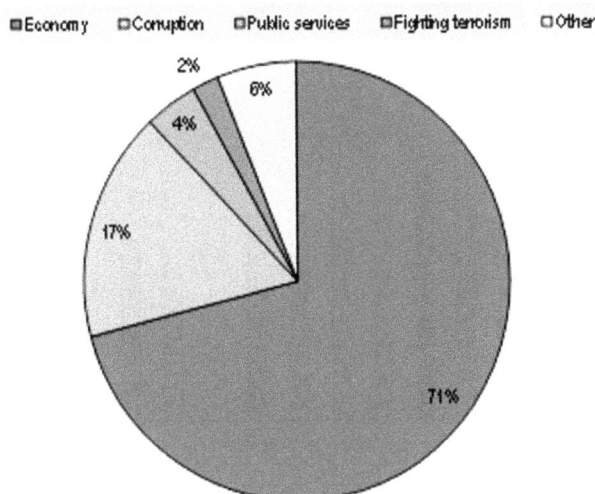

Source: Arab Barometer (2019), Jordan Country Report, https://www.arabbarometer.org/countries/jordan/

Combatting growing perceptions of corruption

Growing perceptions of corruption in the public sector, and the perceived inability of policy makers to counter these instances, can have a noteworthy effect in disengaging citizens from public life (OECD, 2019). Corruption has been a constant challenge in the MENA Region, and was one of the main catalysts of the Arab Spring uprisings in 2011. Indeed, the 2019 Arab Barometer notes that trust in government has been declining in the region, reaching a record low in Jordan (38%), Lebanon (19%), Morocco (29%) and Tunisia (20%).

Deteriorating trust in Jordan is in parallel taking place in a context of perceived low levels of transparency and public sector integrity. The country ranked 76 out of 151 countries in the transparency of government policy making index and received a score of 65.87% on the rate corruption control (World Bank, 2018). While Jordan provides the public with substantial budget information (63% score), the country provides few opportunities for the public to engage in its development process (11% score)[3] (IBP, 2017). In parallel, Jordan has remained consistent in regards to Transparency International's Corruption Perception Index[4], with an average score of 48 since 2016 and ranking 60th globally in 2019 (Transparency International, 2020). Within the region, however, Jordan ranks sixth among 18 countries on this index and remains above the regional average score (39) (See Figure 1.3).

Figure 1.3. 2019 Transparency International Corruption Perception Index

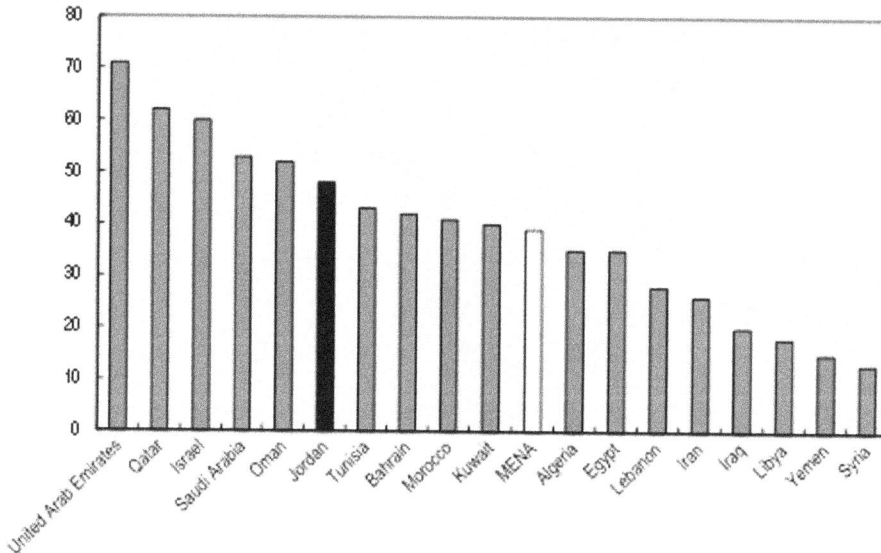

Source: Transparency International (2020), Corruption Perception Index 2019, Berlin, https://www.transparency.org/cpi2019 (Accessed online on 11/02/2020).

Following the Arab Spring, His Majesty King Abdullah II signed a royal decree establishing the National Integrity Charter and its executive plan to enhance national integrity systems[5]. The plan consolidates His Majesty's comprehensive vision for reform under 168 commitments on the need to institutionalize governance, rule of law, combatting corruption, and public participation in the decision-making process. Jordan's commitment to strengthening integrity systems was also emphasized in the context of the decentralization reform through the National Renaissance Plan (2019-2020)[6]. Its vision for transformation acknowledges combatting corruption and enhancing transparency and integrity as critical factors to strengthen institutions in light of the decentralization of power to the sub-national level.

Embedding the principles of transparency, integrity and accountability are at the core of promoting a culture of open governance. As such, streamlining current national gains to governorates and municipalities in Jordan can help regain the public's trust and deter scepticism around decentralization. Indeed, the involvement of citizens in the needs assessment process can serve as a counterweight to hold authorities accountable, as well as to ensure that advocated needs are reflected in local development plans.

Engaging a young and unevenly distributed population in Jordan

Based on the 2015 Jordan Population and Housing census, the overall population in Jordan consists of approximately 9.5 million individuals, of which a third are non-Jordanians. The population, however, is unevenly distributed across governorates, with 75% of all inhabitants concentrated in Amman (4 million), Irbid (1.77 million) and Zarqa (1.36 million) respectively (OECD, 2017) (See Figure 1.4). The current efforts to decentralize power by fostering local planning can thus serve as an opportunity to refocus attention and address the needs of less-populated regions.

Figure 1.4. Most densely populated cities in Jordan

Source: World Population Review (2020), Jordan Population 2020, available online at: http://worldpopulationreview.com/countries/jordan-population/

Jordan is also one of the youngest countries in the world, with more than one-third of the population aged between 12-30 years (OECD, 2018). However, the current socio-political and economic environment is negatively affecting youth political participation, civic engagement and access to economic opportunities (Milton-Edwards, 2018). Despite high education attainment rates, young people in Jordan have low prospects for job opportunities. Youth apathy in public life is also on the rise, as illustrated by the low voter participation (35%) from the 17-30 age group in the 2016 legislative elections (Milton-Edwards, 2018).

The Renaissance plan thus recognizes the important role of youth in the successful implementation of decentralization. Under its objective to "Develop political life and safeguard public freedoms," the government of Jordan seeks to "integrate youth in public decision making in municipalities through the process of decentralisation and governorate councils". The plan also aims to develop programmes to strengthen the ability youth to participate in public life by developing a democratic culture, citizenship, and enrooting pluralism in society. Ensuring the effective implementation of these efforts targeting youth, at a time with growing discontent from citizens, will be key to forge the country's path towards socioeconomic development.

Addressing population shifts: Refugees and emigration

The crises in neighbouring Iraq and Syria have propelled the arrival of refugees to Jordan over the course of the last 15 years. In 2019, UNHCR recorded approximately 747,080 refugees in the country, with a significant share (83.5%) primarily living in urban areas. The vast majority of refugees come from Syria (654,692) and are concentrated in Jordan's most densely populated governorates, including Amman (29.5%), Mafraq (24.8%) and Irbid (20.6%) respectively (See Figure 1.5). This influx has strained public service delivery and raised concerns around ensuring the long-term socio-economic integration of this group.

Figure 1.5. Distribution of Syrian Refugees in Jordan across the 12 governorates

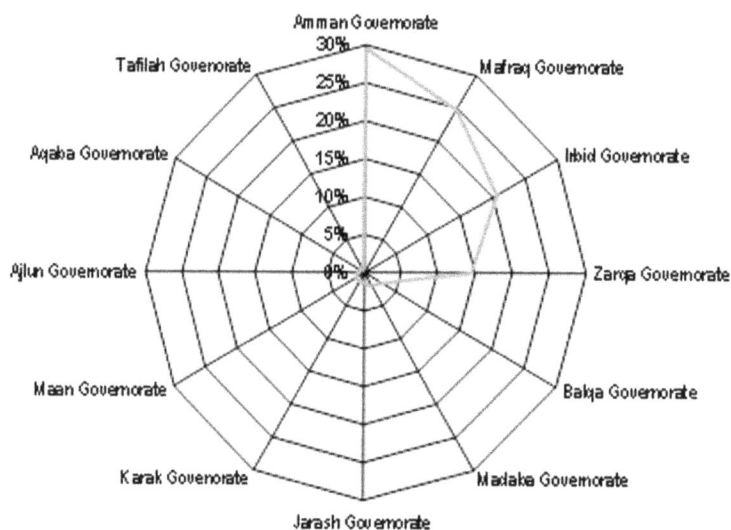

Source: UNHCR (2020), Syria Regional Refugee response portal, accessed online on 16/01/2020, https://data2.unhcr.org/en/situations/syria/location/36

In parallel, the state of the economy is prompting Jordanians to seek opportunities outside of the country. According to the Arab Barometer (2019), almost half of the population (45%) has expressed interest in emigrating, twice the rate from 2016. Findings from this report also identified strong links between migration and youth, with over 59% of those willing to leave the country falling between the ages of 18-29. These sentiments are indicative of the need to engage the Jordanian society, beyond the usual suspects.

The Decentralization Reform in Jordan

Over the past decade, Jordan has undergone a series of reforms in efforts to respond to its evolving economic, social and political landscape. Notably, transformations to Jordan's multi-level governance structures did not happen in a vacuum, but rather as part of a series of robust democratic reforms.

In the aftermath of King Abdullah II's rise to power in 1999, His Majesty introduced a series of political and economic reforms promoting the liberalization of markets. In his first letter to then Prime Minister Abdul Rauf Al-Rawabdeh, the King stressed the need to "enhance national unity, promote democracy, strengthen the judiciary, boost efficiency in the public sector, and strengthen the role of the media in promoting freedom of expression" (Muasher, 2011). The "Jordan First" national vision, introduced subsequently in 2002, consolidated these aspirations, and as a result, over 211 new laws were adopted in the following years. Of notable mention is the enactment of the 2007 Access to Information Law, which was the first of its kind in the MENA region.

In parallel, Jordan was the first country in the region to join the Open Government Partnership. Responding to these calls for change, King Abdullah II established a Royal Committee and a National Dialogue Committee, whom led the amendment of over 42 articles in the Constitution (OECD, forthcoming). These efforts culminated in the *Jordan 2025* vision, with over 400 prerogatives to improve the welfare of citizens as well as service design and delivery, amongst which decentralization featured prominently. In his letter on March 2014, the King stressed the importance of promoting local governance with the primary goal of ensuring a "just distribution of development gains by giving priority to governorate development programmes" (OECD, 2017a). As a result, the government introduced a series of laws in 2015 reforming elections, political parties (No.39)[7], decentralization (No. 49) and the role of municipalities (No. 41).

The 2015 Decentralization Laws

The approval of the 2015 Decentralization and Municipalities Laws marked an important milestone to ground the country's ambitions in bringing local governments closer to citizens. The Decentralization Law established the Executive and elected Governorate Councils and outlined broadly their roles and prerogatives. The law also governs the election process and the authority of these new actors. Moreover, the Municipalities law formalized existing governance mechanisms and assigned municipal stakeholders a role in local development planning, in particular through the collection and transfer of citizens' needs to the Governorate level. As outlined by the previous OECD (2017) report "*Towards a New Partnership with Citizens: Jordan's Decentralization Reform*", the Government of Jordan centres its decentralization reform on four key pillars:

- Promoting stakeholder participation to support local development;
- Promoting sustainable local development and an equal distribution of benefits;
- Improving the efficiency and effectiveness of service delivery within local administrations and municipalities; and
- Improving efficiency in the planning and preparation of Governorate budgets.

Acknowledging decentralization as a continuous process, the Legal and Administrative Committees in Parliament conducted a National Dialogue in 2015, seeking citizens' feedback to identify potential amendments for both 2015 draft laws. It also sought to activate the role of the permanent committees in Parliament, address existing gaps regarding electoral rules, and enhance public participation in the decision-making process, in alignment with His Majesty's vision (Al Hayat, 2020). Overall, the National Dialogue exhibited high participation levels with a total of 4,160 attendees from civil society, academia and various political parties. A total of 746 recommendations were brought forward - namely 103 on the draft Decentralization Law, 124 on the draft Municipalities Law and 519 general observations on the functioning of Municipalities and Governorates (Al Hayat, 2020).

The Government of Jordan also included concrete actions to support the implementation of the 2015 laws under its 3rd OGP National Action Plan (2016-2018). Under Commitment 5, the Government of Jordan pledged to issue the requisite regulations and instructions to implement the Decentralization Law and hold Governorate Council Elections in 2017. Its ambition stated that: "by involving public participation in economic and development decisions, the Government's aim is for the decentralization path, and the practical encouragement it entails, to constitute a direct input in improving the government's performance and its proximity to the public which will allow the public to effectively and more transparently monitor government performance" (OGP, 2016). This commitment was overseen by the Ministry of Interior and MoPIC.

The rollout of the Decentralization Reform in Jordan (2017 – 2020)

In 2017, the Government of Jordan established the Inter-Ministerial Committee on Decentralization and the Executive Committee as the oversight bodies guiding the implementation of the 2015 Decentralization and Municipalities laws. The Inter-Ministerial Committee, which is composed of six Ministries led by the Minister of Interior[8], is responsible for providing guidance on seven domains of the decentralization reform, including: "legislation, institutional capacity, awareness raising, institutional and organizational structures, evidence and procedures, financing, local development and services and information technology (Kahdim, 2018)". In addition, the Executive Committee is in charge of overseeing the implementation of the decentralization legislation and is responsible for preparing local elections in Jordan.

Guided by the Executive Committee, the country held its first local elections on the second half of 2017, where over 6,000 candidates competed for more than 1,833 seats on 100 city and town councils and 12 new governorate councils (Reuters, 2017). According to the Independent Election Commission (IEC), the elections yielded a low voter turnout rate (31.71%) out of 1,302,949 eligible citizens, which was however higher (by 6.5%) than previous municipal elections in 2013. The highest voter turnout rates per Governorate were registered in Ajloun (62.8%), Mafraq (59.8%), Karak (57.14%) and Jerash (56.91%), while the lowest was accounted for in Amman (17.56%) (Al Emam, 2017).

The 2017 elections were marked for having, for the first time, two types of elected councils. Notably, elections saw the establishment of 12 elected governorate councils, where previously, members concerned with the administration of governorates were appointed by the Ministry of the Interior in consultation with the Parliament. With the 2015 Decentralization law, the total number of seats in Governorate Councils was set to 380, from which 32 seats were assigned to women (quota of 20-25%) and 45 (a quota of around 15%) for appointments by the Cabinet. These new institutional arrangements at the sub-national level aimed to set the foundations for materializing King Abdullah II's aspirations for decentralization to be centred on stakeholder participation.

Following the establishment of Local and Governorate Councils in late 2017, the first needs assessment cycle for the design of sub-national development plans was conducted until the second quarter of 2018. The process involved consultations with citizens carried out by 355 local councils in 100 municipalities (Kahdim, 2018). Needs collected in 2018 were primarily focused on health, education and public roads policies. Building on the lessons learnt, a second needs collection process was carried out in 2019 to identify local development projects under the overall 2019 budget of 300 million Jordanian dinars (close to 400 million USD) for all 12 Governorates.

The Administrative Committee of the Parliament, in cooperation with the Ministry of Political and Parliamentary Affairs, conducted a second National Dialogue in 2019 on an umbrella of political reforms – namely on decentralization, elections and political parties. The National Dialogue aimed at reviewing and evaluating the implementation mechanisms around the decentralization law, in particular the mandate and authorities of Governorate Councils. In total 43 sessions were organized with 1,568 members of civil society, academia and public institutions across the 12 governorates (Al Hayat, 2020). The main conclusions of the National Dialogue highlighted the need to:

- Merge the decentralization and municipalities law into a single law and set clear responsibilities between Municipal and Governorate actors (including the Local Council as well as the Executive and Governorate Councils);

- Strengthen the powers and authority of Governorate Council. In addition, establish coordination mechanisms with Governorate Department Directors to aid in the implementation of local development projects.

- Clarify the relationships between Governorate Councils and Executive Councils, as well as between Governorate and Local Councils. The need for better coordination between these actors and with key Ministries was also highlighted;

- Develop a legal environment that encourages partnerships between local authorities and the private sector;

- Support the implementation of development projects by encouraging foreign and local investments, with a focus of supporting projects beyond those concentrated in Amman. Participants also highlighted the need to address the lack of or insufficient financial resources for the implementation of local development projects;

- Raise awareness around the opportunities for participation in the needs assessment process, as well as broader results in the context of decentralization to regain trust across the 12 governorates; and

- Develop the capacities and tool for members of the Governorate and Local Development Units to perform their work, in particular to engage stakeholders in the development of local policies.

Responding to the main concerns raised around the decentralization reform, the Government of Jordan presented to Parliament a new draft *Local Administration Law* in early 2020. The new legislation proposes to merge the 2015 Decentralization and Municipalities laws, following an evaluation of the main legislative, administrative and technical challenges facing decentralization. Some of the tenants up for debate include the quotas and composition of Governorate Councils, new powers for Municipal and Governorate actors, as well as updated procedural requirements for sub-national authorities carrying out the needs assessment process.

Overall, the Government of Jordan faces a challenging road ahead in making these reforms more visible to citizens, whilst overcoming economic and political difficulties. The general sense of discontent in the country has led to four government reshuffles since mid-2018 alone, indicating a relatively volatile political moment for the country. The ongoing decentralization process should thus use the new momentum brought about by the new law to revamp initiatives at the local level, in particular to offer new opportunities for participation in the design and delivery of policies and services. At the same time, the ongoing COVID-19 crisis underlines the imperative for better communication, coordination, and cooperation between the central and local levels of government in order to ensure the delivery of vital services and the rebuilding of economic livelihoods across the country.

Methodology of this report

To support Jordan's efforts to embed the principles of transparency, integrity, accountability and stakeholder participation at the local level, this report analyses the current gaps in the needs assessment and development planning process. It is based on a survey developed by the OECD to understand the extent to which local needs are identified in a participatory manner and whether they are reflected in the budgeting and development planning processes. In 2019, MOPIC distributed the survey to 54 sub-national government representatives and 30 civil society organizations (See Box 1.3 for more information).

This publication is also based on desk research and extensive interviews conducted with a wide variety of stakeholders during multiple fact-finding missions. A workshop with over 50 national, governorate and municipal stakeholders was also carried out to validate the data and the main findings of this report. Furthermore, this review incorporates the outcomes discussed in meetings in the framework of the 2019 National Dialogue and complements the work carried out by other donor organizations on the ground.

Box 1.3. Data collection for the Open Government at the Local Level Review of Jordan

The survey was given to local, municipal and governorate stakeholders from across Jordan, including 8 out of 12 governorates. Respondents included elected members of governorate and municipal councils, mayors as well as officials from development units at all three levels. Participants to this survey include representatives from: The Amman Governorate; Madaba Governorate; Zarka Governorate; Mafraq Governorate; Tafilah Governorate; Ma'an Governorate; Jerash Governorate; Ajloun Governorate; Tafila Municipality; Battir District; Salt Municipality; Ajloun Municipality; Jaresh Municipality; Zarka Municipality Mafraq;

A second survey was also conducted to 30 civil society organization in Jordan. Participants to this survey include representatives from: Rasheed; Opinions without borders for sustainable development; Community Media Network; Qudurat Association for Community Development; Change agents for sustainable development; Virtue Charity Association; Jordan Legal Network; We Rise Center; Tomorrow's Youth Center; Namaa Development and Capacity Building; Bashayer Al Nour Charity Associatiom; Madaba Tomorrow for development and training; Our Children's Future Cultural Association; The Creatives Association to support students and the local community; Sons of Al Khalil Association for solidarity; and Ain Rasun Charity Association.

Source: Author's own work

References

Al Hayat – RASED (2020), Background Note on Decentralization in Jordan.

Al Emam (2017), Voter turnout rate higher by 6.5% than that of previous local polls — IEC, published online on the Jordan Times, https://www.jordantimes.com/news/local/voter-turnout-rate-higher-65-previous-local-polls-%E2%80%94-iec

Arab Barometer (2019), Jordan Country Report, https://www.arabbarometer.org/countries/jordan/

Economic Policy Council of Jordan (2017), Jordan Economic Growth Plan (2018-2022), available online at: http://extwprlegs1.fao.org/docs/pdf/jor170691.pdf

Jordan Times (2019), Jordan's economic growth projections for 2019 drop slightly to 2.2%available online at: https://www.jordantimes.com/news/local/jordans-economic-growth-projections-2019-drop-slightly-22

Jordan Times (2019), Unemployment continues to rise in 2019, hitting 19%, available online at: https://www.jordantimes.com/news/local/unemployment-continues-rise-2019-hitting-19

Kandah, A. (2019), Decentralisation: a complex puzzle or a conflict between ministries?, Opinion piece in the Jordan Times, https://www.jordantimes.com/opinion/adli-kandah/decentralisation-complex-puzzle-or-conflict-between-ministries

Kardoosh (2019), Jordan Struggles to Reverse Decades of Poor Economic Management, available online at: https://www.haaretz.com/opinion/.premium-jordan-struggles-to-reverse-decades-of-poor-economic-management-1.7804160

Middle East Monitor (2019), Government survey: Extreme poverty in Jordan at 15.7%, available online at https://www.middleeastmonitor.com/20190409-government-survey-extreme-poverty-in-jordan-at-15-7/

Milton-Edwards, B. (2019), Marginalized youth: Toward an inclusive Jordan, published by Brookings online at: https://www.brookings.edu/research/marginalized-youth-toward-an-inclusive-jordan/

OECD (2019a), *Making Decentralisation Work: A Handbook for Policy-Makers*, OECD Multi level Governance Studies, OECD Publishing, Paris, https://doi.org/10.1787/g2g9faa7-en.

OECD (2017a), *Towards a New Partnership with Citizens: Jordan's Decentralisation Reform*, OECD Public Governance Reviews, OECD Publishing, Paris, https://doi.org/10.1787/9789264275461-en.

OECD (2017b), *Recommendation of the Council on Open Government*, OECD, Paris, https://www.oecd.org/gov/Recommendation-Open-Government-Approved-Council-141217.pdf

OECD (2016), *Open Government: The Global Context and the Way Forward*, OECD Publishing, Paris, https://doi.org/10.1787/9789264268104-en.

UNICEF (N.D.), *Social protection in Jordan*, https://www.unicef.org/jordan/social-protection

UNHCR (2020), *Syria Regional Refugee response portal*, accessed online on 16/01/2020, https://data2.unhcr.org/en/situations/syria/location/36

The Kingdom of Jordan's Department of Statistics (2019), *Jordan Population and Family Health Survey 2017-18*, https://www.dhsprogram.com/pubs/pdf/FR346/FR346.pdf

World Bank (2020a), *US$374 Million to Provide Cash Assistance to Poor and Vulnerable Households in Jordan*, available online at: https://www.worldbank.org/en/news/press-release/2020/06/25/us374-million-to-provide-cash-assistance-to-poor-and-vulnerable-households-in-jordan

World Bank (2020b), *MENA Crisis Tracker*, available online at: http://documents1.worldbank.org/curated/en/280131589922657376/pdf/MENA-Crisis-Tracker.pdf

World Bank (2019), *Jordan's Economic Update*, Washington D.C, https://www.worldbank.org/en/country/jordan/publication/economic-update-october-2019

World Bank (2017), *Country data on Transparency of Government Policy Making*, TCDATA360, Washington D.C., https://tcdata360.worldbank.org/indicators/h7da6e31a?country=BRA&indicator=688&viz=line_chart&years=2007,2017

World Bank (2018), *Country data on Control of Corruption*, TCDATA360, Washington D.C, https://tcdata360.worldbank.org/indicators/hf0ef1ed3?country=BRA&indicator=369&viz=line_chart&years=1996,2018

UNHCR (2019), *Jordan Fact Sheet*, available online at https://data2.unhcr.org/ar/documents/download/71536

Notes

[1] Jordan 2025 is the 10-year national vision and strategy of Jordan. This document features more than 400 policies and procedures promoting a participatory approach between the government, civil society and businesses.

[2] Extreme poverty considers all those living with less than $1 dollar a day.

[3] The IBP considers countries that score above 60 on the Open Budget Index as providing sufficient budget information to enable the public to engage in budget discussions in an informed manner. IBP Open Budget Index: 0 being low and 100 being very transparent.

[4] CPI score: 0 being highly corrupt and 100 being very clean

[5] Royal Committee to Enhance the National Integrity System (2012). National Integrity Charter and Executive Plan to Enhance the National Integrity System. Amman, Jordan. See: Link

[6] Jordan Renaissance Plan (2019 – 2020), https://your.gov.jo/

[7] https://www.ilo.org/dyn/natlex/natlex4.detail?p_lang=en&p_isn=103043

[8] Members of the Inter-Ministerial Committee include: Minister of Municipal Affairs, Minister of Planning and International Co-operation, Minister of Public Sector Development, Minister of Finance, Minister of Telecommunications and Information Technology, and Minister of Political and Parliamentary Affairs.

Chapter 2. Good governance enablers in the Needs Assessment Process

This chapter analyses how governance structures in Jordan have responded to the drastic transformation brought about by the decentralization reform. It looks into the country's efforts to clarify roles and responsibilities, support co-ordination, strengthen strategic planning and ensure adequate human and financial resources. This chapter also identifies concrete avenues for governance structures to better support stakeholder participation in the needs assessment process, in light of the new Local Administration Law in drafting.

Fostering good governance enablers at the local level in Jordan

The decentralisation reform in Jordan raised public expectations that policies and services would be brought closer to local communities through new channels for stakeholder participation. Indeed, important milestones were achieved following the adoption of the 2015 Municipalities and Decentralization laws, including the 2017 local elections, the establishment of the *Inter-Ministerial* and *Executive Committees*[1] and two successful rounds of the needs assessment cycles. Despite this progress, several challenges remain to continue the process of decentralization, by integrating local stakeholders and ensuring their needs are reflected in the overall planning process.

Notably, Jordan has embarked on an ambitious reform agenda to deconcentrate power to the Local, Municipal and Governorate levels. The 2015 Municipalities (No. 41) and Decentralization (No. 49) Laws established new governance structures for public institutions involved in the decentralization process. These structures consider the preparation and approval of needs lists, which are "tabulated lists of development needs and associated projects generated at local community level, consolidated by municipal and/or administrative authorities and then passed on to Governorate Councils for approval and budget allocation" (Khadim, 2018).

The laws also established elected councils at the Governorate and Municipal level to foster this new participatory and bottom-up approach. Local Development Units at the Municipal (LDUs) and the Governorate level (GDUs) were also mandated to act as the general secretariat at the governorate and municipal level and as the interface with local community stakeholders, civil society and private sector. Together with the Governor and the Mayor, these actors form the public sector architecture of the decentralization reform more broadly (see Figure 2.1).

Figure 2.1. The Public Sector Architecture of Decentralization

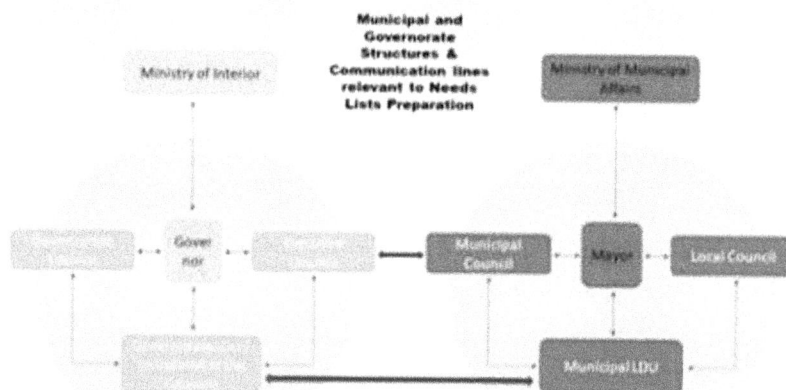

Source: Khadim, M. (2018), Political Economy Analysis of Jordan, developed within the framework of the USAID project Cities Implementing Transparent, Innovative and Effective Solutions (CITIES).

The laws also include a general description of the process to collect needs and build local development plans. At its early stages, consultations are organized by Local Councils to identify a relevant list of needs and potential projects, which is subsequently shared with the respective Municipality. Headed by the Mayor, the Municipal Council, with support from the LDU, filters and reviews the list, develops the municipal needs assessment document and transfers it to the Governorate level. In this third phase, the GDU filters and consolidates the needs manual, which is used by the Executive Council – headed by the Governor -

to draft development plans and propose budgetary allocations. The final needs list is then shared with the Governorate Council who is in charge of the final approval and budget allocation (See Figure 2.2).

Figure 2.2. The collection and approval process of needs

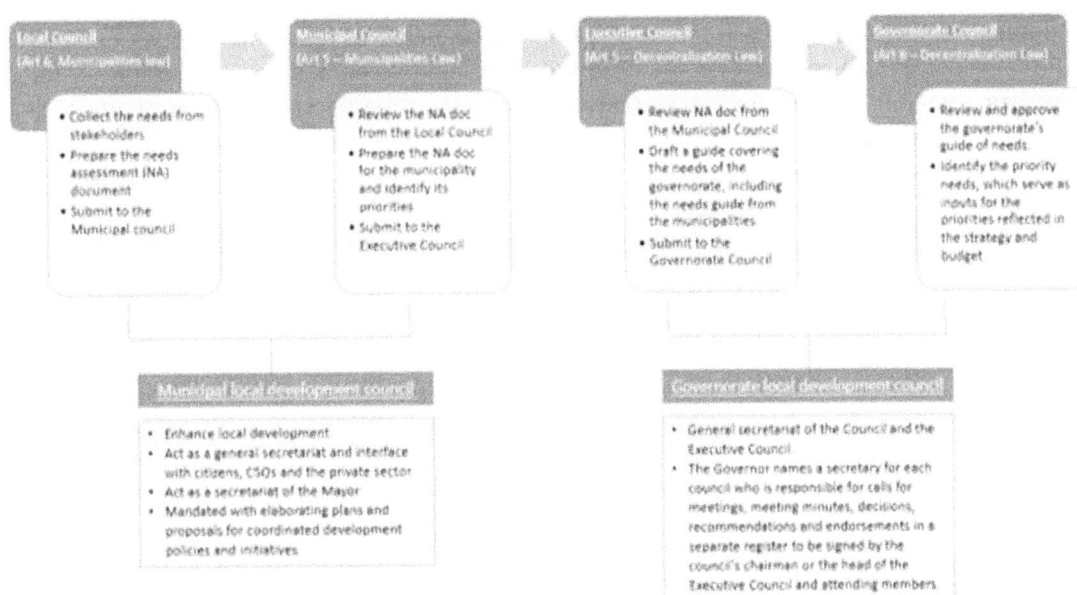

Local Council (Art 6, Municipalities law)
- Collect the needs from stakeholders
- Prepare the needs assessment (NA) document
- Submit to the Municipal council

Municipal Council (Art 5 – Municipalities Law)
- Review the NA doc from the Local Council
- Prepare the NA doc for the municipality and identify its priorities
- Submit to the Executive Council

Executive Council (Art 5 – Decentralisation Law)
- Review NA doc from the Municipal Council
- Draft a guide covering the needs of the governorate, including the needs guide from the municipalities
- Submit to the Governorate Council

Governorate Council (Art 6 – Decentralisation Law)
- Review and approve the governorate's guide of needs
- Identify the priority needs, which serve as inputs for the priorities reflected in the strategy and budget

Municipal local development council
- Enhance local development
- Act as a general secretariat and interface with citizens, CSOs and the private sector
- Act as a secretariat of the Mayor
- Mandated with elaborating plans and proposals for coordinated development policies and initiatives

Governorate local development council
- General secretariat of the Council and the Executive Council
- The Governor names a secretary for each council who is responsible for calls for meetings, meeting minutes, decisions, recommendations and endorsements in a separate register to be signed by the council's chairman or the head of the Executive Council and attending members

Note: In some Governorates, there is also the contribution of "administrative authorities" in parallel to that of the Municipal Council (Kadhim, 2018).
Source: Author's own work, based on the 2015 Decentralization and Municipalities laws and Kadhim (2018).

As noted in the OECD report "*Towards a New Partnership with Citizens: Jordan's Decentralisation Reform*", however, the laws do not include a major transfer of powers to sub-national levels of government, accountability lines are still blurred and the roles for local non-governmental stakeholders in the needs assessment process remain undefined (OECD, 2017a). In fact, the OECD found that "the articles dedicated to governance structures, functions, funds and multilevel co-ordination barely represent 25% of the tenants within the Decentralization Law (12 articles out of 47) and 41% of the Municipalities Law (32 of 77 articles) respectively". As OECD analysis shows, these issues have remained relevant in the law's current phase of implementation.

Acknowledging that decentralization is a dynamic process - from which the country is still at the early stages of its implementation - a new draft *Local Administration Law* was presented to Parliament in early 2020 following an evaluation of the main legislative, administrative and technical challenges facing decentralization. Resulting from a series of national dialogues in 2019, the new legislation aims to merge the 2015 Decentralization and Municipalities laws. Some of the proposed changes introduced by the new law include the quotas and composition of the Governorate Councils, new powers for Municipal and Governorate actors, as well as updated procedural requirements for sub-national authorities carrying out the needs assessment cycle. The new legislation is expected to enter into force in 2020.

On 9 May 2019, furthermore, Jordanian Prime Minister Omar al-Razzaz announced a third cabinet reshuffle and established the Ministry of Local Administration (MoLA) (previously known as the Ministry of Municipal Affairs) to oversee the activities of Municipal and Governorate Councils. This change granted MoLA a leading role in the decentralization process and the authority to support the work of municipal and local authorities.

Against this backdrop, a focus on good governance enablers is all the more important with recent developments drastically transforming the role of sub-national authorities in the decentralization process. Indeed, pre-existing challenges have been exacerbated by the COVID-19 pandemic, where capacity and resource gaps, coupled with high levels of citizen distrust, are posing threats to the effectiveness of response and recovery measures.

While progress has been achieved in terms of the implementation of recommendations outlined in the OECD (2017) report in this regard, findings note room for improvement in terms of clarifying roles and responsibilities, fostering an effective strategic planning cycle, strengthening inter-institutional dialogue and ensuring adequate skills and financial resources in local administrations (See Figure 2.3). Indeed, local governments have struggled to adapt to the profound and rapid reorganization of structures resulting from the 2015 laws, citing the lack of or insufficient incentives (70%), financial (70%) and human resources (57%) as the top three bottlenecks to the operational effectiveness of the needs assessment process.

Figure 2.3. Main governance related challenges facing sub-national authorities to engage stakeholders in the needs assessment process

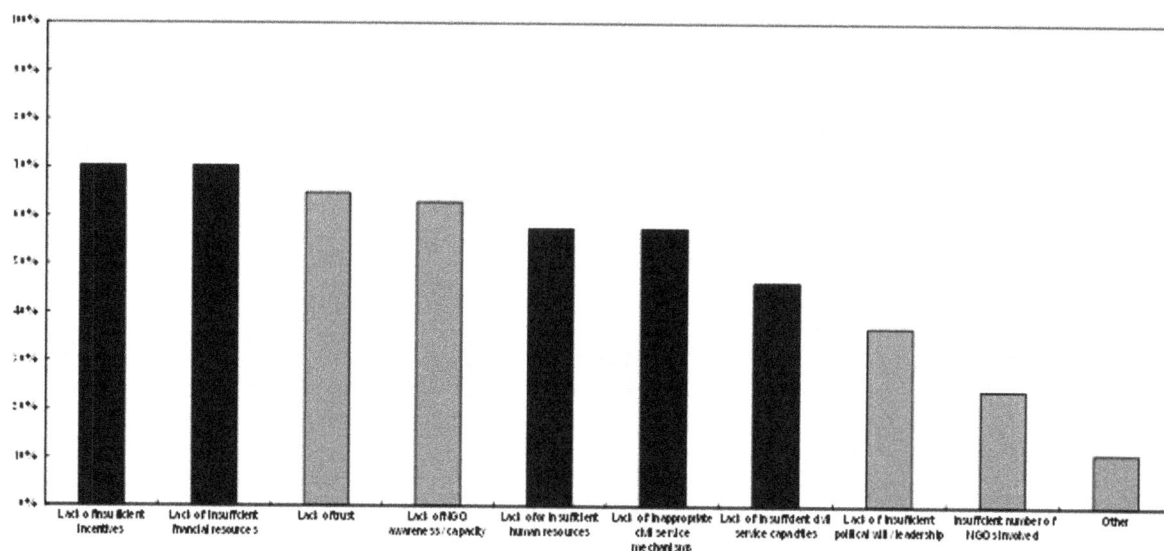

Source: OECD (2019) Questionnaire for sub-national governments: Stakeholder participation in Jordan's needs assessment process.

This chapter will therefore assess the five aforementioned challenges in more detail and identify avenues to contribute toward a more open and participatory needs assessment cycle in Jordan.

Clarifying the overall structure and organization of the Needs Assessment Process

Duplicate and unclear roles and responsibilities, in particular between central and local levels of government, are one of the main challenges in OECD countries implementing decentralization reforms (OECD, 2019a). Lack of clarity can make service provision and policymaking costlier, increase the existence of process bottlenecks and create delays. Unclear and overlapping tasks may also have a negative effect on stakeholder participation, by creating confusion among citizens on which institution is responsible for a specific service and by blurring accountability lines (Allain-Dupré, 2018).

Thus, to make decentralization work, governments should "clarify the responsibilities assigned to different government levels" and ensure that sub-national level functions are codified in significant detail within legal and regulatory frameworks and widely disseminated (OECD, 2019a). Such functions refer to each institutions' roles regarding standards, human resources, financing, service provision, information sharing, engagement, monitoring and evaluation, among others. Regarding the need to clarify roles – and of particular relevance for Jordan – several OECD members, such as Japan and the Netherlands, have engaged in a series of reforms to clarify central and local government competencies (see Box 2.1).

Box 2.1. Unitary states' efforts to clarify roles and responsibilities at the local level

- **Japan (1999):** the country adopted the 1999 decentralisation law, which sought to eliminate opaque central decision-making on local responsibilities and clarified competencies more generally. Subsequent waves of reform have continued to focus on promoting greater municipal autonomy, clear delineation of responsibilities, and proper financing.
- **The Netherlands (2012 – 15):** The 2012 decentralisation reform aimed to reallocate competencies between the levels of government, in particular by empowering provincial and municipal actors and by establishing a simpler and clearer division of responsibilities, avoiding the overlapping of functions.

Source: OECD (2019), Making Decentralisation Work: A Handbook for Policy-Makers, OECD Multi level Governance Studies, OECD Publishing, Paris, https://doi.org/10.1787/g2g9faa7-en.

As a result of the 2017 elections, Jordan is in the process of setting institutional structures to support the bottom-up approach to the collection of needs from local communities. OECD survey data shows that a majority of sub-national governments (80%) have a person, unit or department in charge of stakeholder participation activities in the needs assessment process (see Figure 2.4). These structures often refer to LDUs and GDUs, which are mandated to engage local stakeholders and support Municipal and Governorate Councils with economic development activities and the implementation of new investment projects.

Figure 2.4. Do you have a person, unit or department in charge of stakeholder participation?

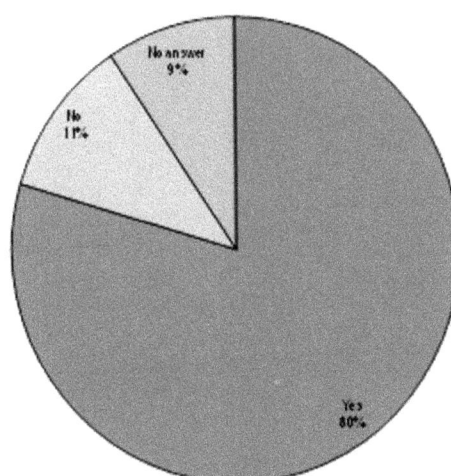

Source: OECD (2019) Questionnaire for sub-national governments: Stakeholder participation in Jordan's needs assessment process.

44 |

Guidelines have also been developed with the aim of increasing civil service mechanisms to carry out needs assessment process. In 2017, the Ministry of Local Affairs (MoLA) developed the "Procedures Manual for Preparing Municipal Needs" followed by the "Guide of the strategic and operational plans for the governorate within the decentralization framework" published by the Ministry of Interior in 2018 (see Box 2.2 & Box 2.3). These guidelines have been increasingly disseminated across the 12 Governorates, as a majority of OECD survey respondents (70%) declared to have guidelines or instructions supporting their process of assessing needs (see Figure 2.5).

Figure 2.5. Q8. Does your office have guidelines or instructions for staff designed to support the needs assessment process?

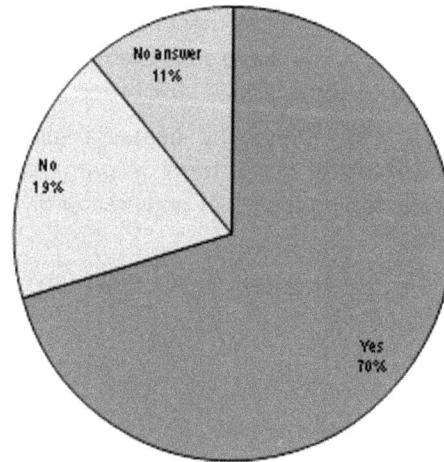

Source: OECD (2019) Questionnaire for sub-national governments: Stakeholder participation in Jordan's needs assessment process.

Box 2.2. Procedures Manual for Preparing Municipal Needs in Jordan (2017)

The Procedures Manual for Preparing Municipal Needs and Development Plans is a practical guide tool that enables Municipal and Local Councils to achieve some of the outputs stipulated by the Municipalities Law. Among its objectives, it seeks to establish a methodology aimed to promote community participation in preparing Municipal Development Plans.

In order to facilitate the task of these Councils, the manual includes three milestone phases, each of which meets the output required by the law. It also includes an introductory section as well as a preparatory phase with ex-ante related considerations.

- **Phase I:** refers to the preparation and approval of the Municipal Needs list. This phase includes planning procedures, the management of needs identification sessions with the Local Community and the approval of Municipal Needs.
- **Phase II:** refers to the preparation and approval of development plans, including budget costs. This phase includes procedures for determining project priorities, procedures to prepare and approve development plans, as well as tools to estimate costs for their inclusion in the Municipal budget.
- **Phase III:** refers to the follow-up of projects approved in the Municipal Development Plan. This phase included procedures for preparing follow up reports, procedures for sharing the results of work progress with Local Councils and Local Community and management procedures of citizens' complaints.

Source: Ministry of Municipal Affairs, Jordan (2017), Procedures Manual for Preparing Municipal Needs.

Box 2.3. Guide of the strategic and operational plans for the governorate within the decentralization framework in Jordan (2018)

The Ministry of Interior developed this guide to provide technical assistance to governorate and executive councils, and in particular local development units, in the preparation of local development plans and collection of needs. The guide describes the overall process and steps in the preparation of local plans, including:

1. The collection and analysis of information;
2. The formulation of the overall vision of local development;
3. The strategic local development plan of the governorate;
4. The medium-term activities of the plan;
5. The annual operational plan;
6. The implementation of the plan; and
7. The review and evaluation of the plan.

Source: Ministry of Interior (2018), Guide of the strategic and operational plans for the governorate within the decentralization framework, accessed on 14 July 2019.

While Jordan has made progress in setting institutional structures, there is yet room to clarify roles and responsibilities. In fact, OECD interviews noted that the exact roles, responsibilities and activities for GDUs and LDUs are unclear or not fully broken down. Moreover, the organizational charts of both LDUs and GDUs differ significantly across governorates, and the distinction of roles between municipal and governorate units remain blurred. Beyond this lack of vertical alignment, there is also a need to clarify the relationship between members of Executive Councils and Governorate Councils.

OECD interviews also noted that while most Governorates have guidelines, the lack of capacities and resources of LDUs and GDUs impede these actors from carrying out technical tasks (i.e. consultations, cost benefit analysis and evaluation). In some cases, due to this technical barrier, sub-national actors refer to the law as their sole guiding document. Additional analysis has found that "while guides were useful and fairly easy to use by stakeholders, certain sections related to project priority and impact weighing were hard to comprehend or apply... and links to relevant legislation could be improved" (Khalid, 2018). Thus, to increase buy-in and incentives to carry out procedures, in particular more technical tasks (i.e. cost benefit analysis, data sharing), guidelines should be accompanied by capacity building activities to build an understanding of the decentralization process at all levels.

With the introduction of the new local administration law, there is also an opportunity to revamp the support that will be provided by the MoLA to Municipal and Governorate Councils. These new measures could consider codifying specific tasks and sub-tasks within the law, as well as building new guidelines with detailed information on procedures. In particular, the relationship between all actors of the decentralization architecture should be clarified. Indeed, the effective implementation of the new law will require the awareness raising of all sub-national actors on the new tenants contained therein, and the efficient equipment of sub-national authorities for its implementation.

To capture the opportunities to respond to the His Royal Majesty's vision to place citizens at the heart of local decision-making, MoPIC and the MoLA should emphasize strengthening stakeholder participation in the needs assessment process (see Box 2.4 for an OECD template for clarifying responsibilities). Making sure that decentralization lives up to the growing expectations of citizens would also entail defining clear mechanisms for the four stages of the needs assessment process - namely, planning, budgeting, implementation and impact evaluation. In addition to existing guidelines, a centralized information repository with all resources, including a process mapping of the needs assessment process, could further support the alignment of procedures.

Box 2.4. OECD Guideline: Clarifying responsibilities assigned to different government levels

The OECD toolkit includes a checklist template with several elements to consider when assigning roles and responsibilities to central and local level institutions, including elements such as:

Guideline 1. Clarify the responsibilities assigned to different government levels			
Checklist	Yes	Partially	No
Legislative powers of various orders are clearly demarcated by: • Constitution • National legislation • Other (executive orders, agreements) • All of the above?			
For shared functions, is there clarity in the division of powers: • Who sets the policy • Who decides on the standards • Who is responsible for oversight • Who is responsible for financing • Who is responsible for service provision • Who produces the service • Who monitors and evaluates service delivery • How do citizens provide feedback			
For each of the shared functions and sub-functions, are there institutional mechanisms in place for: • Consultation/co-ordination • Burden sharing • Conflict resolution			
Sub-functions within each function are decentralised to a similar extent			
Subnational governments are empowered to pursue integrated approaches to local economic development			
There is a separation of decision making for capital and operating expenditures			
The authority to hire, fire and set terms of reference and day-to-day management/supervision for own employees rests at the same level for each function			
There a separation of decision making among various levels on planning, policy, finance and provision for each function			

Source: OECD (2019), Making Decentralisation Work: A Handbook for Policy-Makers, OECD Multi level Governance Studies, OECD Publishing, Paris, https://doi.org/10.1787/g2g9faa7-en.

Ensuring greater multi-level coordination and transfer of information via the Needs Assessment process

The successful take-up of ambitious reforms, such as that of decentralization, requires establishing vertical and horizontal mechanisms and processes of intergovernmental consultation, co-operation and joint decision-making, as well as an open and regular communication (OECD, 2019a).

In this context, the OECD recognizes the role of co-ordination to embed stakeholder participation at the local level. The OECD Recommendation of the Council on Open Government (2017b) argues that governments should "coordinate, through the necessary institutional mechanisms, open government strategies and initiatives – horizontally and vertically – across all levels of government to ensure that they are aligned with and contribute to all relevant socio-economic objectives". As part of the open state provision (number 10), the Recommendation also recognizes the role of local government in pushing the open government agenda, notably for initiatives to reach all relevant stakeholders.

Most OECD countries have developed both formal and informal co-ordination mechanisms between central and sub-national levels of government. Indeed, platforms for vertical co-ordination have been established in 11 OECD countries (i.e. on matters involving environment, infrastructure, transport, technology and development), and 14 countries mandate national governments to consult sub-national governments prior to the adoption of new regulation (OECD, 2017c). Other coordination mechanisms typically used include dialogue platforms, partnerships or contracts across levels of government and co-financing arrangements (see Box 2.5).

Box 2.5. Examples of multi-level coordination in OECD countries

1. The Local Government Commission in New Zealand:

The Local Government Act created an independent and permanent body on local reform issues in 2002 with the aim of strengthening relationships across levels of government. The Commission includes three members appointed by the Minister of Local Government. Its main task is to decide on the structure of local government and on electoral arrangements for local 78 authorities in New Zealand (11 regional councils and 67 territorial authorities).

2. Multi-stakeholder Fora in Nordic countries:

Regular formal meetings held between representatives from central and local government, in particular in associations of local governments (Norway, Finland, Sweden, etc.). SNG associations are consulted on any legislative changes influencing sub-national government and participate in the dialogue and negotiations with the central government.

Source: Local government commission of New Zeland (N.D), The role of the commission, accessed on 9 August 2019, http://www.lgc.govt.nz/the-role-of-the-commission/; OECD (2019), Making Decentralisation Work: A Handbook for Policy-Makers, OECD Multi level Governance Studies, OECD Publishing, Paris, https://doi.org/10.1787/g2g9faa7-en.

In Jordan, the government created an Inter-Ministerial Committee and an Executive Committee to promote horizontal coordination in the implementation of the decentralization reform. Both Committees bring together the ministries that play a key role in the decentralisation reform – notably the Ministry of Planning and International Cooperation, the Ministry of Interior, the Ministry of Municipal Affairs, the Ministry of Public Sector Reform and the Ministry of Finance. Vertical coordination between national public entities and Governorate and Municipal Councils, however, is managed by the Ministry of Interior and MoLA respectively.

Based on the country's decentralization priorities defined in the Jordan 2025 vision, notably seven thematic sub-committees emerged from the Inter-Ministerial Committee:

- Subcommittee on the legislation;
- Subcommittee on the institutional, structural and organizational process and manuals;
- Subcommittee on institutional capacity;
- Subcommittee on finances;
- Subcommittee on local development and public services;
- Subcommittee on public awareness; and
- Subcommittee on information technology.

Through these thematic groups, the Inter-Ministerial and Executive Committees have accomplished important milestones. Notably, these Committees have issued by-laws and instructions to implement the Decentralization Law, for instance the By-law of Governorate Councils' Constituencies, which regulates the work of the Governorate Councils, sets procedures for meetings and for its internal elections. The work of the Committees has also supported the setting of financial ceilings for governorate budgets, as well as the needs guide and strategic and operational plans guide for municipalities and governorates.

In addition, discussions within the framework of the *National Dialogue* have served as a space for sub-national authorities to discuss pertinent reforms to the laws. The 2019 National Dialogue, coordinated by the Ministry of Parliamentary and Political Affairs and the Economic and Social Council (ESC), consisted of 43 sessions carried out across the country. Local level stakeholders, together with civil society, engaged in discussions on an umbrella of political reforms – namely, decentralization, elections and political parties – with a particular focus on the structure of Governorate Councils, as well as their mandates and authorities.

While the creation of co-ordination structures at the national level via the Inter-Ministerial Committee, the Executive Committee and the National Dialogue are important steps, there is room to foster the integration of local and municipal actors in a more systematic way. In particular, sub-national co-ordination mechanisms, both horizontal and vertical, have yet to be developed.

Indeed, the crosscutting nature of the needs assessment process, in addition to the new architecture of decentralization, have transformed working relationships between local actors. While Article 3.3 of the decentralization law mandates that the "governor is to co-ordinate between the governorate council and the municipalities and other sub-national stakeholders", there is still a lack of clarity in terms of channels and common procedures for submitting local development proposals, for example (OECD, 2017a).

The lack of procedures or co-ordination mechanisms have exacerbated information gaps between local, municipal and governorate councils in the construction and implementation of needs lists and more broadly. Notably, lack of feedback regarding the final needs considered for the development plan and budget was identified as the main disconnect between the three levels. In fact, data from a CITIES political economy analysis shows that three governorates – Ma'an, Jerash and Madaba – stated that Executive Councils did not inform municipalities about the final 2018 need lists before this was transmitted to the Governorate Council for its approval (CITIES, 2018). Local public officials also noted to the OECD that information is shared on an informal basis and its availability depends to a large extent on personal relationships, which may help explain the information sharing disparities throughout the 12 Governorates.

In addition to instances of low willingness or capacity to share information, process barriers may also act as inhibitors of multi-level co-ordination. Findings from OECD fact-finding missions suggest that there are also coordination challenges between Governorate Councils and Executive Councils, in particular when approving the final list of needs. Administrative barriers, such as process bottlenecks and short time frames to conduct the needs cycle, seem to have a spill over effect of hindering co-ordination opportunities with municipal and local levels.

Building the capacity of Governorate and Executive councils to incorporate inputs from lower levels is also critical to the successful establishment of co-operation mechanisms. Notably, OECD data shows that a significant share of sub-national authorities (41%) did not receive guidance on how to incorporate the needs list developed from lower levels in 2018 (see Figure 2.6).

Figure 2.6. Share of sub-national authorities receiving guidance from the national government on incorporating the needs assessments developed from lower levels

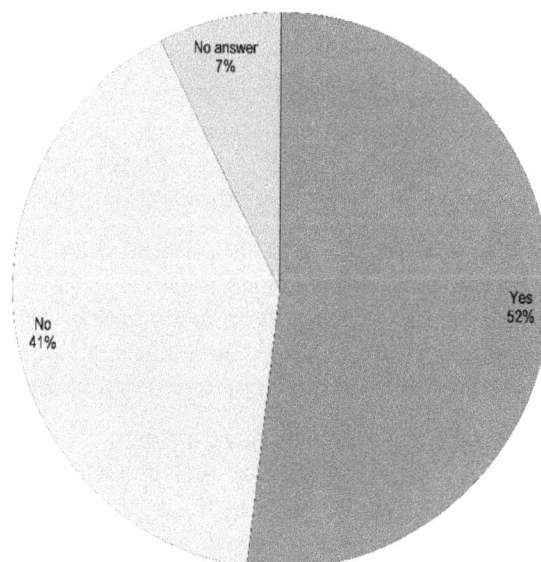

Source: OECD (2019) Questionnaire for sub-national governments: Stakeholder participation in Jordan's needs assessment process.

Against this backdrop, a first step toward establishing co-ordination structures and to more effectively transferring information will entail clarifying procedural requirements. In this regard, Local, Municipal and Governorate Councils could be mandated, for example, to publish their need list documents online. In addition, the Governorate and Executive Councils could be tasked to develop and share a follow-up report detailing the final approved list, budget allocations and the status of implementation of local projects. There is also an opportunity to complement guidelines with concrete standards and planning mechanisms between the three levels, in order to ensure responsiveness to the requirements of the timeframe of the needs assessment budget cycle.

In parallel, the national administration, through the efforts of the Executive Committee and the MoLA, could support the establishment of sub-national co-ordination mechanisms. Such mechanisms could take the form of a local level forum or informal thematic networks to align needs within governorates, share lessons learned and promote cross-fertilization of skills. In some OECD countries, these networks evolve into national associations of subnational governments (see Box 2.6 for the example of COSLA).

Fostering an effective strategic planning cycle in the Needs Assessment process

Strategic planning can also be a key instrument to encourage citizen participation in local decision-making.
It fosters processes that aim to achieve consensus on policies and services and encourages partnerships
to propose, implement and evaluate local projects (United Cities and Local Governments, N.D.). Promoting
stakeholder participation in planning, however, requires local governments to integrate citizens' needs
through the diagnosis, development, management and evaluation stages of the planning cycle.

In addition to the decentralization reform, Jordan has established a comprehensive multi-level strategic
planning framework (see Table 2.1). At the national level, Jordan 2025 sets a ten-year vision to promote
greater socio-economic development. In particular, the strategy acknowledges that active civic
engagement and political participation are central for a democratic culture to emerge at the local level
(OECD, 2017). Under this vision, the Renaissance plan (2019 – 2020) sets a concrete path for the political,
economic and social development of Jordan. To transform these commitments into action, MoPIC leads
and coordinates strategic planning at the central and sub-national level.

Table 2.1. Jordan's strategic planning framework

	Instruments
National level	- **Jordan 2025:** The 10-year national vision and strategy of Jordan. This document features more than 400 policies and procedures promoting a participatory approach between the government, civil society and businesses. - **Renaissance Plan (2019 – 2020)**: Annual government plan outlining national priorities. The Renaissance plan seeks to achieve progress in terms of the state of law, economic productivity and social development towards the achievement of a "human state".
Governorate level	- **Governorate strategy and executive plan:** Annual plan developed by each of the 12 governorates containing local development projects and budget allocations. - **Governorate needs and priorities manual**

Municipal level	• **Municipality needs and priorities manual**
Local level	• **Needs and priorities list**: collected directly from citizens

Source: Author's own work.

Strategic planning at the sub-national level follows a bottom-up approach with the aim of encouraging the alignment and coherence of plans at different levels. Notably, each Governorate develops their own annual strategy and executive plan, proposing concrete investment projects with the support of GDUs and the Executive Council. Municipalities feed into this process by submitting their own Municipalities Needs Manual based on the priorities lists developed by Local Councils. In addition, GDUs provide technical support to the Executive Council throughout the strategic planning process by collecting relevant data, analyzing potential avenues for reform and preparing relevant documents for the decision making process. MoPIC and MoLA provide technical support through trainings and manuals to support work in this regard.

While the development of governorate plans has benefited from the iterative learning of two need cycles, some of the key challenges identified by the OECD (2017) remain. Findings from the OECD survey note that the uptake of this participatory process has advanced but is yet uneven, as 28% of respondents consider that stakeholder contributions are not reflected in governorate plans (see Figure 2.7). Against this backdrop, it will be paramount for the Government to ensure that the approved Local Development Plans reflect the needs and concerns from municipalities and local stakeholders. To support this process, GDUs and LDUs should be equipped with technical skills to translate local needs to medium-term strategic planning. The confluence of many actors in local matters makes it critical to align sub-national and national strategies to ensure that all development needs – from large and small communities – are reflected.

Figure 2.7. Share of sub-national representatives noting whether they feel the contributions made by stakeholders are considered in the needs assessment process

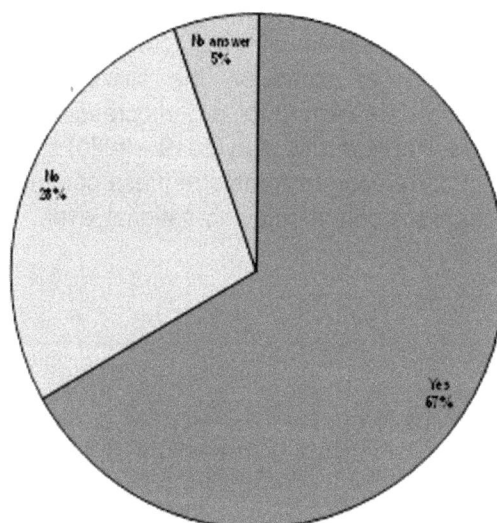

Source: OECD (2019) Questionnaire for sub-national governments: Stakeholder participation in Jordan's needs assessment process.

Beyond the development of plans, efforts could also focus on improving the link between local development projects, their financing and implementation. Fact-finding interviews noted the need for more coordination between Executive and Governorate Councils. Moreover, as the implementation of projects are carried out by a sectoral ministry, the link with Governorate Departments could be further strengthened. Given the complex nature of this process, GDUs could play an important role in bridging the gap between sectors. The creation of procedures and guidelines for local strategic planning could also be developed to support this complex process and align efforts across governorates. New South Wales, for example, developed a strategic planning toolkit to coordinate action across levels of government (see Box 2.7).

Box 2.7. The Strategic Planning Toolkit of the Government of New South Wales

The Government of New South Wales in Australia developed a toolkit to provide guidance on local plan making and to assist in the implementation of the goals and directions contained within nine Regional Plans, a Metropolis of three cities and the five district plans. The Strategic Planning Toolkit applies to all stages of planning, including policy directions for plan making and mapping standards and requirements.

As new planning strategies transpire, the Strategic Planning Toolkit is updated to serve as the centralized one-stop-shop resource for local councils and planning professionals alike to employ best practice planning across New South Wales.

Source: Government of New South Wales (N.D), Strategic Planning Toolkit, https://www.planning.nsw.gov.au/Plans-for-your-area/Local-Planning-and-Zoning/Strategic-Planning-Toolkit

---

In this regard, the Tanmiah System developed in early 2020 by the Ministry of Interior and UNDP could help local actors promote a more transparent and evidence-driven strategic planning process across the needs cycle. This tool notably seeks to "to integrate government's planning process with project implementation through the automated tracking of goals and related measures while providing a means for public feedback" (UNDP, 2020). The Tanmiah System consists of three main components (Ibid). First, a geographic database with over 400 socio-demographic measures is meant to inform policy decisions in real time. Second, the tool provides a project management dashboard for public officials to track relevant information on an initiative's timeline, completion rate and budgets, Lastly, its public relations management (PRM) system gives citizens the ability to submit service requests, review project proposals and provide online feedback in real time on local investment initiatives. At the time of writing, it is not clear the degree of its utilization across all Governorates in Jordan. However, efforts to support strategic planning could benefit from the ample dissemination and adoption of this tool by all relevant local, municipal and governorate authorities in the framework of the needs assessment process.

There is also room to improve the monitoring and evaluation of local development plans. While GDUs are tasked to deliver evaluation reports through a new tool called "Adat Altanmyah", this process is not active in all Governorates. Public officials noted during validation workshops the lack of screening of local development projects in some Governorates, as well as the ad hoc and informal nature of evaluations. To illustrate, 20 hospitals in the Ma'an governorate were allocated despite this number going beyond the national standards of beds per population. Therefore, MoLA, together with MoPIC, could support the institutionalization of ex ante and ex post evaluation processes and promote the take up of the Adat Altanmyah tool. Promoting evaluation processes would foster greater accountability of government departments to development programmes, inform subsequent needs assessment cycles and showcase results to citizens.

Ultimately building more effective participation mechanisms could help communities articulate a vision for its development and generate a sense of ownership. At the national level, the government could help ensure that local needs are connected to broader strategic planning goals and help identify relevant donor-led development opportunities. At the local level, beyond yearly exercises, consultations should inform mid-term and long-term development strategies and programmes. Overall, the aim of the strategic planning process at the sub-national level should aspire to move from the collection of wish lists to the creation of a more structured approach to development and strategic planning. Strengthening the capacities and skills of public servants to conduct stakeholder participation activities in the needs assessment process

Strengthening the capacities and skills of public servants to conduct stakeholder participation activities in the needs assessment process

Ensuring adequate levels of human resources and capacities is critical to the work of sub-national governments. Indeed, as decentralization reforms assign news tasks for local authorities to perform, there is increasing emphasis on enhancing uniform capacities across regions. The OECD Recommendation of the Council on Public Service Leadership and Capability emphasises the importance of ensuring adequate levels of skills to ensure the transformation of a political vision into concrete services (OECD, 2019b). In that context, the OECD developed a framework that identifies the skills needed by public servants to face the increasing complexity, interconnectedness and openness in the public sector.

According to the OECD Recommendation of the Council on Public Service Leadership and Capability, one of the four main areas of skills needed are those related to civil servants' work with citizens. As civil servants provide service delivery, directly to and with citizens, fostering their engagement skills is key to implementing policies and reforms effectively (see Box 2.8). Despite the importance of working with citizens, however, OECD evidence finds the lack of knowledge and skills in this area as one of the main challenges faced by public servants (OECD, 2017d).

Thus, the OECD Recommendation summarises 14 principles to foster a value-driven, trusted, capable, responsive and adaptive public service, suggesting governments invest in civil service capabilities by:

- Continuously identifying skills and competencies needed to transform political vision into services that deliver value to society;
- Attracting and retaining employees with the skills and competencies required;
- Recruiting, selecting and promoting candidates through transparent, open and merit based processes;
- Developing the necessary skills and competencies by creating a learning culture and environment in the public service; and
- Assessing, rewarding and recognising performance, talent and initiative.

Box 2.8. Skills needed for citizen engagement and service delivery

The 2017 OECD Report, Skills for a High Performing Civil Service, summarises the skills needed for citizen engagement and service delivery as:

Strategic orientation	Using engagement skills to achieve specific outcomes to inform, for example, better targeted interventions, such as healthier eating habits or smoking reduction.
Professional expertise	Traditional building blocks of service and engagement skills include professionals with expertise in public relations, communications, marketing, consultation, facilitation, service delivery, conflict resolution, community development, outreach, etc.
Innovation capabilities	Innovation skills applied to engagement to expand and redesign civil service mechanisms through, for example, co-creation, prototyping, social media, crowdsourcing, challenge prizes, ethnography, opinion research and data, branding, behavioural insights/nudging, digital service environments and user data analytics.

Source: OECD (2017), Skills for a High Performing Civil Service, OECD Public Governance Reviews, OECD Publishing, Paris, https://doi.org/10.1787/9789264280724-en. OECD (2019), Recommendation of the Council on Public Service Leadership and Capability, OECD, Paris, https://legalinstruments.oecd.org/en/instruments/OECD-LEGAL-0445.

From an open government perspective, the third provision of the OECD Recommendation of the Council of Open Government urges governments to provide "public officials with the mandate to design and implement successful open government strategies and initiatives, as well as the adequate human, financial and technical resources…" (OECD, 2017b). In fact, a survey of open government reforms in OECD countries found the lack of or insufficient capacity of public human resources as one of the main challenges to implement open government initiatives (OECD, 2016).

Human resource management in Jordan is also one of the main challenges in the needs-assessment process. OECD survey findings identified the lack of or insufficient human resources (57%), existing mechanisms (57%) and capacities (46%) as the key bottlenecks cited by sub-national representatives. Respondents also noted that LDUs and GDUs are lagging in terms of skills to carry out their new functions as a result of the rapid rollout of the decentralization reform. Notably, building capacities at the local level is a common challenge in most OECD countries, as it was encountered for example in the design of infrastructure projects signalled by two thirds of surveyed OECD sub-national authorities (OECD, 2015).

While guidance and trainings are provided, findings suggest a mismatch with current skill gaps, in particular as capacities vary significantly across large and small governorates. As seen in Figure 2.8, a majority of sub-national governments declared that they received trainings (69%) to build stakeholder participation related skills. Even with the existence of these trainings, public officials highlighted during interviews the difficulty of carrying out the needs cycle.

Figure 2.8. Percentage of trainings provided with the express purpose of building capacity to work with stakeholders in the needs assessment process

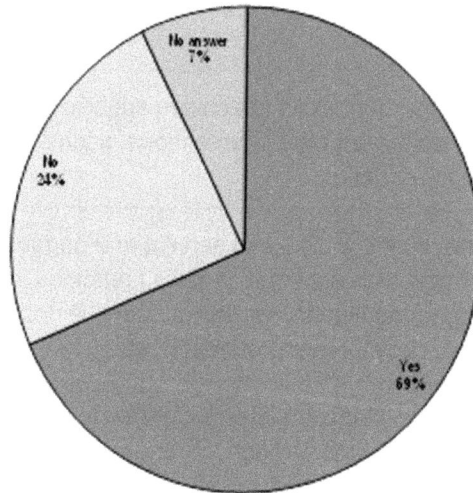

Source: OECD (2019) Questionnaire for sub-national governments: Stakeholder participation in Jordan's needs assessment process.

Despite the provision of trainings by several actors in Jordan, a systemic approach is needed to ensure the coordination, relevance and long-term sustainability of these efforts. According to OECD survey results, local governments received trainings from multiple sources, such as donor organizations (50%), national government ministries (44%) or local/national NGOs (40%) (see Figure 2.9). However, interviews noted that capacity building is mostly conducted on an ad-hoc basis and focuses primarily on technical assistance. Indeed, challenges in Jordan persist as trainings are often dispersed and carried out in isolation without a concrete policy or programme supporting their institutionalization.

Figure 2.9. Main sources of trainings for sub-national level stakeholders in the context of the needs assessment process

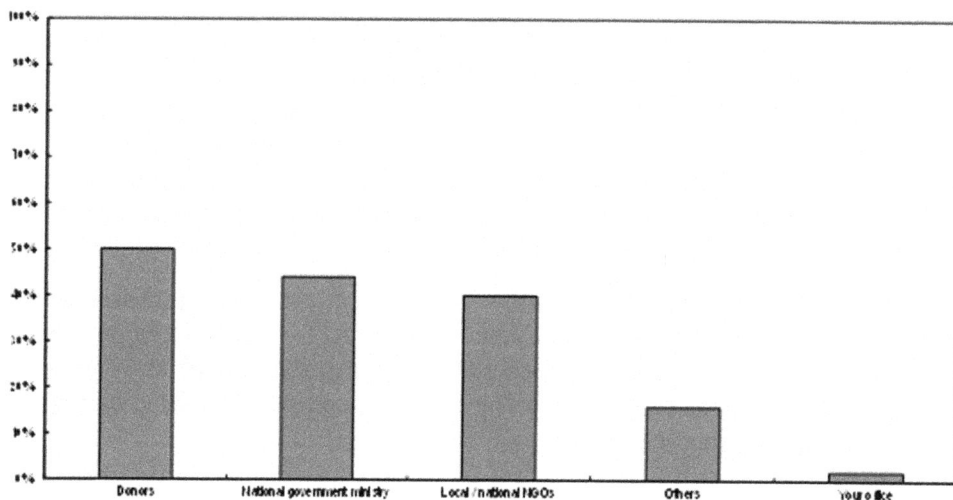

Source: OECD (2019) Questionnaire for sub-national governments: Stakeholder participation in Jordan's needs assessment process.

In light of its role, MoLA could therefore help address these challenges by identifying capacity gaps to better adapt guidance and trainings to the actual needs of different local administrations. Mapping skill gaps across the 12 governorates would allow MoLA to provide relevant and tailored technical trainings (i.e. evaluation, cost benefit analysis, etc.). These trainings could also be translated into institutionalized programs targeting local civil servants, in particular from LDUs and GDUs. Trainings could also focus on building and managing a number of transparency and accountability tools, such as open data portals, citizen budgets, community planning and participatory budgeting. For their effective implementation, the Government of Jordan could consider coordinating with the Institute of Public Administration.

In addition, MoLA could adopt a coordinating role to explore partnerships with other relevant stakeholders (i.e. CSOS, donors) and better assess local capacity needs. Creating a joint catalogue of available options could, for example, foster a more targeted and comprehensive approach for trainings. In addition, the institutionalization of capacity building efforts into programmes or academies (see Box 2.9) could be explored. The goal of Jordan's capacity building efforts should ultimately focus on promoting their reach, relevance and sustainability.

Box 2.9. Public service academies for regions and municipalities

- Chile's Capacity Building Academy for Municipalities and Regions

In 2007, Chile created *the Academia de Capacitation Municipal y Regional SUBDERE* to support the implementation of the country's decentralization reform. The academy provides a set of technical standards for municipalities and regions and supports a broad spectrum of knowledge that can be adapted to different local realities. Within its offer, the academy provides in-person training programmes, expert panels as well as online MOOCs. A key success factor of the academy's programmes relies in the close relationships with members of academia, civil society and donor organizations.

- Maryland Academy for Excellence in Local Governance

In partnership with the Maryland Municipal League, the University of Maryland developed a programme on municipal governance. This programme is voluntary and open to all local officials in Maryland. The academy provides in-person and online classes on Risk Management; Conducting Effective Meetings; Consensus and Team Building; Employment Issues; Ethics; Municipal Budgeting; Implementing the Public Information Act; Structure of Municipal Government and conducting open and participatory meetings.

- The Latvian School of Public Administration (LSPA)

Established in 1993, the LSPA provides high-quality training and consultation services to meet the current and future needs of public servants at both the national and local level. The training and services developed by the LSPA help ensure high quality of public service in Latvia, with specialized courses aimed at Municipalities. The LSPA has designed a training module system that contains around 120 different courses.

Sources: Author's own work based on online content. See http://www.academia.subdere.gov.cl/?page_id=8, https://spp.umd.edu/your-education/executive-development/state-and-local-government/academy-excellence-local-governance and www.vas.gov.lv/en/.

Financial resources for sub-national governments need to match the new functions laid out in the decentralization reform in Jordan and the expansion of the roles and responsibilities of local governments. Adequate financing is of particular importance as sub-national authorities become increasingly responsible for the delivery of many crucial services.

Notably, the OECD Open Government Recommendation recognizes the need for governments to provide adequate human and financial resources to implement open government strategies and initiatives successfully (OECD, 2017b). Beyond the absolute amounts allocated to support open government initiatives, countries must ensure that funding sources are clear and consistent (OECD, 2016).

The sources for funding open government initiatives vary across governments. In fact, funding for these initiatives in more than half of OECD countries (52%) comes from a combination of sources (OECD, 2016). Resources may come from a single central body, from the body responsible for its implementation or from external stakeholders. The latter may include, for example, the private sector, donors, multilateral organisations or other organisations such as NGOs or the European Commission.

Securing financial resources remains a key challenge in most OECD countries. OECD data shows that most member countries identify a lack of necessary financial resources as one of the main challenges, both to coordinate (43% of OECD countries) and to implement (49% of OECD countries) open government strategies and initiatives (OECD, 2016).

More broadly, challenges persist with low levels of available funding for local development projects within governorates, and the limited autonomy for governorate budget allocations. The total allocated budget for decentralization for the years 2018, 2019, 2020 and 2021 constitutes 3% of the country's annual budget (Kadhim, 2018). Placing this numbers in perspective, the 2019 Governorate Council Budget amounted to 300 million Jordanian Dinars (close to 400 million USD), from which the General Budget Department allocated an expenditure limit to each governorate. On this basis, proposed local development projects were selected by the Executive Council and approved by the Governorate Council. However, Governors can only make decisions on projects of less than JOD 100,000 (around 142,000 USD)[2].

Despite of the new responsibilities granted to municipalities through the 2015 laws, general funding streams in Jordan remain limited for these actors. Municipal budgets (excluding that for the Greater Amman Municipality) are heavily dependent on a transfer allocation system based on a number of socio-economic factors, including population. Overall, mayors have expressed concerns about the lack of predictability in the system, as budget allocations tend to fluctuate significantly across years, in particular with growing strains to the economy. Indicative of this low levels of funding, OECD survey results also found that 70% of sub-national authorities suffer from a lack of or insufficient financial resources to implement decentralization related activities. Low financing levels may have the adverse effect of lowering the capacity and incentive of local development units to carry out needs assessment activities, as well as discouraging participation and thus perpetuating a general sense of distrust from the public.

The same can be said for the lack of dedicated funding for stakeholder participation activities in all three levels of government. In fact, OECD data shows that only 13% of respondents confirmed having a specific budget for the needs assessment process and only 2% have a budget for broader participation activities (see Figure 2.10 & Figure 2.11). Indeed, municipalities struggle to conduct participation activities as they operate on their own resources and limited funding streams allocated by MoLA. Dedicated funding in this regard is all the more important to support the intermediary role of local governments between the public, the governorate council and the national administration. Access to finance should therefore be consistent with the new functional responsibilities of local authorities to collect needs from and engage with local communities.

Figure 2.10. Share of sub-national authorities with a dedicated budget for the needs assessment process

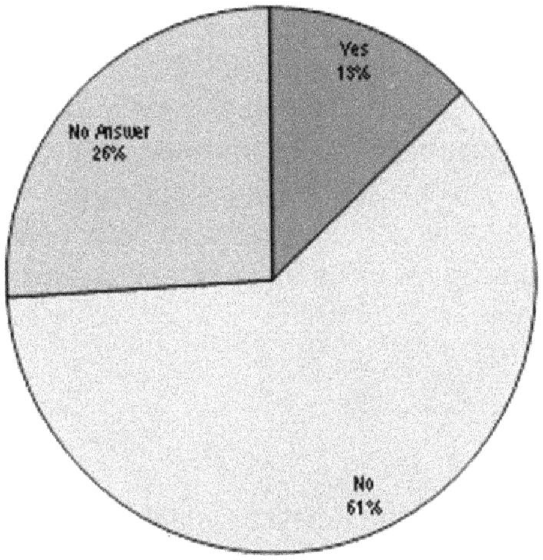

Source: OECD (2019) Questionnaire for sub-national governments: Stakeholder participation in Jordan's needs assessment process.

Figure 2.11. Percentage of sub-national authorities with a dedicated budget for participation initiatives more broadly

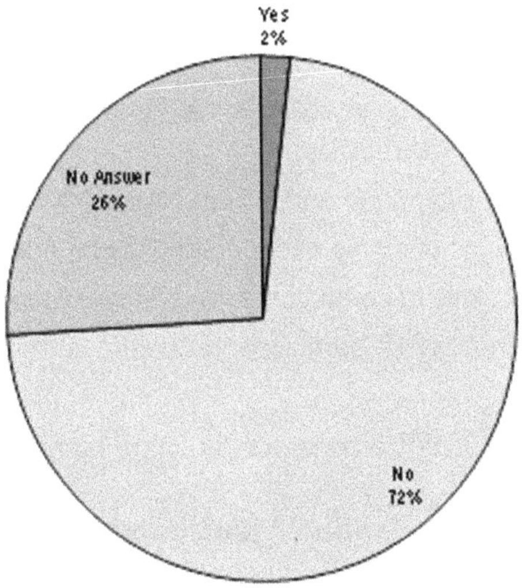

Source: Ibid

Because of this lack of resources, donors play a large role in funding needs assessment meetings. While external funding can make important contributions to participation initiatives, more efforts are needed from all levels of government to ensure the sustainability of participatory activities. Given the challenges in identifying additional funding with the current economic context in Jordan, the Government of Jordan could consider transitioning to a mixed system of funds[3].

The needs assessment process could therefore benefit from establishing a dedicated budget line to provide the necessary resources for participation initiatives and the collection of needs. As the needs assessment process is at the core of the reform, a dedicated-budget line for these activities would strengthen the mandate and capacity of GDUs and LDUs to engage with communities. In addition, having a dedicated budget line could also renew the incentives of public servants to carry out participation activities.

An initial step to address funding gaps would thus require mapping existing and future financing needs in each Governorate to make the case for investments in local development projects. As each governorate has varying fiscal capacities, needs and abilities to provide local public services, this exercise would allow setting realistic budget limits for each region. This analysis should also identify regional and national priorities, unaddressed needs and results of past local development projects. Engaging in a yearly mapping exercise, including the monitoring and impact evaluation of investments, could significantly increase transparency and make the needs assessment process more informed. This is all the more important to strengthen the link between budgetary allocations and strategic planning between the national and local level.

Recommendations

The 2015 rollout of the decentralization reform drastically changed the tasks and responsibilities of local governments in Jordan. Indeed, sub-national authorities, in particular GDUs and LDUs, faced challenges to hone their new role and underwent a difficult "learning by doing" process, were challenges have been further exacerbated by the ongoing COVID-19 pandemic. While the iterative nature of the needs assessment cycles has informed improvements in the process, the quest to meet citizens' high expectations on the promise of decentralization continues.

With local governance structures undergoing a rapid transformation, this chapter identified a number of avenues to strengthen governance mechanisms to promote greater stakeholder participation in the needs assessment cycle, including:

- Clarifying responsibilities and accountability lines for each of the three levels of sub-national government to empower GDUs and LDUs;
- Promoting more effective co-ordination and information transfer across levels of government;
- Fostering an effective strategic planning cycle that builds on stakeholder participation initiatives;
- Strengthening civil servant skills to conduct stakeholder participation activities;
- Ensuring long-term sustainability of participation initiatives at the local level through dedicated financial resources.

To this end, the Government of Jordan could consider the following recommendations:

Clarifying the overall structure and organization of the needs assessment process

- Map the needs assessment process and codify the specific roles and responsibilities of each stakeholder involved. Particularly, clearly differentiate tasks of stakeholders in Municipal, Executive and Governorate Councils, as well as for LDUs and GDUs. Such an activity could be accompanied by new visual material that would clarify roles, promote a coherent vision of the decentralization process and flag opportunities for citizens and civil society to participate.
- Clarify functions and sub-tasks regarding the four main stages of the needs assessment process, namely planning, budgeting, implementing and evaluating for each level of government. Mapping every actor's contributions could also identify potential synergies between the final list of priorities, the strategic plan and the governorate budget.
- Disseminate existing guidelines across stakeholders in each of the 12 governorates more effectively. Consider creating a centralized information repository where all guidelines, training calendars and other relevant information can be found.

- Include concrete procedures and instructions in existing guidelines for local development units carrying out engagement related activities. This could include, for example, establishing procedural requirements to standardize activities throughout municipalities and governorates, such as a required quarterly hearings or annual evaluation reports.

Ensuring greater multi-level coordination & transfer of information via the needs assessment process

- Establish procedural requirements to foster multi-level coordination. This could include mandating local, municipal and governorate councils to make publicly available their needs list documents. Sub-national authorities could also develop and publish a follow-up report on the needs assessment, budget allocations and the status of implementation of local projects.
- Include representatives from Local and Municipal Councils in regular meetings between the Governorate and Executive Councils. This would facilitate coordination and strengthen relationships at the governorate level.
- Establish formal sub-national co-ordination mechanisms, such as a yearly forum between local authorities or thematic communities of practice. These networks could bring together local, municipal and governorate representatives to share experiences, lessons learnt and to identify common challenges and opportunities in pushing the decentralization agenda forward. Establishing a formal mechanism for co-operation would also help institutionalize the relationship between the three levels of government.

Fostering an effective strategic planning cycle in the needs assessment process

- Ensure the reflection of local needs into governorate and national development plans. Efforts should focus on strengthening the technical capacity of GDUs and LDUs to support the participatory nature of the process.
- Strengthen the link between the development of plans, their financing and their implementation. The government could also consider formalizing or regularizing the evaluation of plans to support this process further. In this regard, ensuring the adoption of the Adat Altanmyah tool could support evaluation efforts.
- Support the transformation of the strategic planning process at the sub-national from the collection of wish lists to the creation of a more structured approach through innovative forms of stakeholder participation that promote co-creation. The ample dissemination and adoption of the Tanmiah System across local, municipal and governorate entities could be a first step in this regard.

Strengthening the capacities and skills of public servants to conduct stakeholder participation activities in the needs assessment process

- Assess the capacity challenges to better adapt trainings to the needs of local governments through a mapping of skills gaps across the 12 governorates.
- Design and implement a series of technical training modules (i.e. in areas such as evaluation, cost benefit analysis, etc.) to ensure the necessary capacities and skills at the governorate and municipal levels exist to carry out the needs assessment process.
- Provide technical and specialized trainings to GDUs and LDUs, in particular on how to carry out stakeholder participation related initiatives in the context of the needs assessment process. Trainings could also focus on building and managing a number of transparency and accountability tools, such as open data portals, citizen budgets, community planning and participatory budgeting.

- Explore potential partnerships with other stakeholders, such as NGOs and donors, who also provide trainings related to participation at the local level in order to create synergies. These trainings could also be coordinated with the Institute of Public Administration. In close coordination with NGOs, the government could develop a catalogue of existing trainings and disseminate it across the 12 governorates.

Ensuring the continuity of participation initiatives through dedicated financial resources

- Map the present and future financing needs to set realistic budget limits for each governorate based on available funding. This exercise should assess national and regional priorities, local needs and results from previous budgetary allocations to inform future decision-making, to promote a more transparent process and ultimately build citizen trust in the needs assessment process.
- Allocate and standardize a dedicated budget line in each governorate to carry out participation activities, both in the framework of the needs assessment process and beyond.
- Map the existing pool of external sources of funding that could be leveraged to fund opportunities to engage with stakeholders, build capacity to carry out these activities, ensure sectorial studies match with the proposed needs/projects, etc.

References

Allain-Dupré, D. (2018), Assigning Responsibilities across Levels of Government: Trends, Challenges and Guiding Principles for Policy-makers, OECD, Paris.

Kadhim, M. (2018), Political Economy Analysis of Jordan, developed within the framework of the USAID project Cities Implementing Transparent, Innovative and Effective Solutions (CITIES).

Mahadin E., Binda C. & Khasawneh M. (2018), Legal Review of the Jordanian Decentralization Law, issued by Karak Castle Center for Consultations and Training.

OECD (2019a), Making Decentralisation Work: A Handbook for Policy-Makers, OECD Multi level Governance Studies, OECD Publishing, Paris, https://doi.org/10.1787/g2g9faa7-en.

OECD (2019b), Recommendation of the Council on Public Service Leadership and Capability, OECD, Paris, https://legalinstruments.oecd.org/en/instruments/OECD-LEGAL-0445

OECD (2017a), Towards a New Partnership with Citizens: Jordan's Decentralisation Reform, OECD Public Governance Reviews, OECD Publishing, Paris, https://doi.org/10.1787/9789264275461-en.

OECD (2017b), Recommendation of the Council on Open Government, OECD, Paris, https://www.oecd.org/gov/Recommendation-Open-Government-Approved-Council-141217.pdf

OECD (2017c), Multi-level Governance Reforms: Overview of OECD Country Experiences, OECD Multi-level Governance Studies, OECD Publishing, Paris, https://doi.org/10.1787/9789264272866-en.

OECD (2017), Skills for a High Performing Civil Service, OECD Public Governance Reviews, OECD Publishing, Paris, https://doi.org/10.1787/9789264280724-en

OECD (2016), Open Government the Global Context and the Way Forward, OECD Publishing, http://dx.doi.org/10.1787/9789264268104-en

OECD/CoR (2015), Infrastructure Planning and Investment across Levels of Government: Current Challenges and Possible Solutions, OECD, Paris

UNDP (2020), Faster, Easier and Smarter Service Delivery: This is how Jordan is Localizing the SDGs, available online at: https://www.jo.undp.org/content/jordan/en/home/stories/faster--easier-and-smarter-service-delivery--this-is-how-jordan-.html

United Cities and Local Governments (N.D.), Strategic Urban Planning from a Local Governments'

Perspective, Policy Paper on Strategic Urban Development developed by the Commission on Urban Strategic Planning, https://www.uclg.org/sites/default/files/EN_525_draftpolicypapermonica2504.pdf

Notes

[1] Inter-Ministerial and Executive Committees bring together the ministries that play a key role in the decentralisation reform, including the Ministry of Planning and International Cooperation, the Ministry of Interior, the Ministry of Municipal Affairs, the Ministry of Public Sector Reform and the Ministry of Finance.

[2] https://platforma-dev.eu/wp-content/uploads/2017/03/Mashrek-Decentralisation-in-the-Mashrek-region1-1.pdf

[3] A Mixed system of funds refers to the management of a diverse range of funding streams, including that from donor organizations, national budget allocations, etc.

Chapter 3. The role of public communication in supporting the needs assessment process at the subnational level in Jordan

This chapter analyses the extent to which public communication at the sub-national level in Jordan can contribute to greater transparency and participation, particularly throughout the process to design local development plans and budget. It provides an overview of local communication efforts and explores a series of avenues for subnational authorities to establish a two-way dialogue with citizens around the decentralization reform, its process and outcomes. To achieve this objective, the chapter outlines recommendations to consider, including the establishment of a more strategic communications approach, encourage the implementation of the ATI right at the subnational level, promote the proactive disclosure of information on the needs assessment process and the use of audience insights to tailor messages and channels.

Public communication as a key lever of effective reforms

Public communication can play a fundamental role in bridging the divide between governments and citizens. Separate from political discourse, it allows the public to gain access to relevant information and represents an avenue for citizens to engage with their public administration on issues that matter most to them. This function of government can help build trust, raise awareness around key reforms and change behaviours. The OECD Recommendation of the Council on Open Government recognizes that effective communication can promote greater transparency and participation, making it a key pillar of successful open government reforms (OECD, 2017).

The OECD defines public communication as "any communication activity or initiative led by public institutions for the public good" (OECD, 2020). It can include the provision of information, as well as consultation and dialogue with stakeholders. To reap its full potential, however, governments must transition toward establishing a two-way dialogue with the public (See Figure 3.1).

Figure 3.1. Transitioning from a one-way toward a two-way communication approach

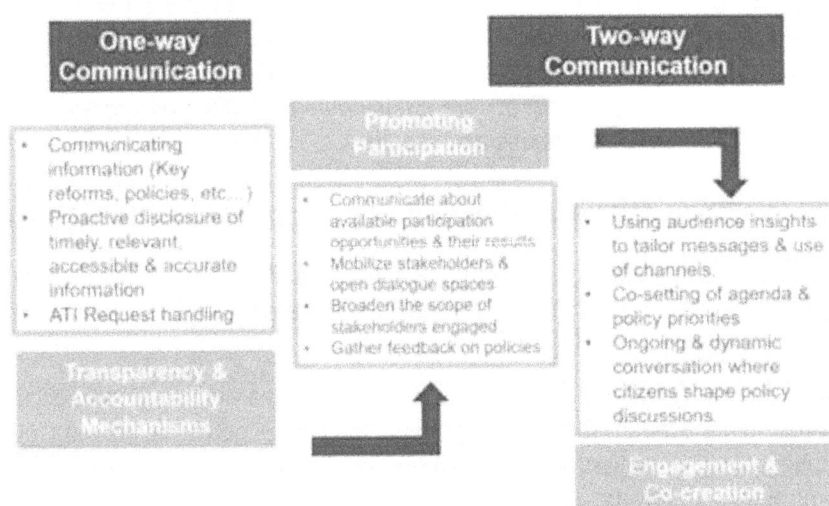

Source: Author's own work

In this regard, communication can be a key pillar of effective local governance by promoting the participation of stakeholders in the design and delivery of policies and services. Firstly, this function can help mobilize stakeholders to engage in public consultations, local hearings and other forms of citizen participation and provide them with the necessary information to contribute to the decision making process. Secondly, it can help provide an open a space where citizens can share their concerns, feedback and proposals for action. Thirdly, communication can help reach a wider variety of audiences and broaden the scope of actors involved beyond the usual suspects. Lastly, it can help regain citizen trust and showcase the value of participation initiatives through the dissemination of information about the entire policy making process, including its outcomes and results.

Finding opportunities to establish more collaborative relationships with the public at the subnational level is particularly important for Jordan to regain citizens' trust, in light of the volatile economic and political landscape in the country. As outlined in chapter 1, trust levels are at an all-time low, where only 38% of the Jordanian population trusts public institutions (Arab Barometer, 2019). In addition, the COVID-19 crisis has underlined how low levels of citizen trust, together with growing instances of mis- and dis-information, can pose threats to the effectiveness of response and recovery measures.

The following chapter provides an overview of the potential of communication to promote participation in the needs assessment process in Jordan. The analysis outlines the key issues facing the new architecture of decentralization to share information across and beyond levels of government and outlines potential avenues to establish a two-way relationship with the public.

Fostering communication with citizens in the needs assessment process in Jordan through a two-way communication

Although information is a necessary precondition for openness, raising awareness around the decentralization process is only the first step. Indeed, to promote meaningful communication, subnational authorities must transition toward the establishment of a two-way dialogue with citizens with a focus on promoting participation in the design of local development plans and budgets. This is of particular relevance as the primary goal of decentralization is to grant subnational governments with the necessary authority to formulate policies and identify service needs autonomously, promote local participation, and increase government performance as per *Jordan's 2025 vision* (OECD, 2017b).

During OECD interviews, however, subnational authorities attributed the lack of communication capacities, tools and mechanisms, together with low levels of public awareness, as some of the main reasons for the stagnant levels of participation in the process to collect local needs. The following section will therefore explore a series of avenues that subnational governments could consider to communicate more effectively around the decentralization reform, its process and results.

Establishing a more strategic communication approach for local governments

Ensuring the effective implementation of ambitious reforms – such as that of decentralization – requires both a strategic and proactive communication approach to raise awareness, facilitate engagement, and generate buy-in among citizens.

In this regard, public communication strategies can help set an overarching approach and establish the direction of initiatives together with short, medium and long-term goals. A growing number of OECD countries are adopting communication strategies at the local level, which answer the "who", "what" and "why" of public communication efforts.

Such strategies should be coupled with communication plans, to operationalize the vision set with details about the "when" and "how" of communication. Plans are also meant to flesh out the general objectives of the entities' communication approach, together with concrete actions, dates and the individuals responsible for its deployment. A growing number of local administrations are adopting communication plans to enable a more strategic approach to engaging with citizens (See Box 3.1 on some examples of communication strategies and plans).

Box 3.1. Examples of communication strategies and plans

Capmbelltown City Council's Communications Management Plan (2017-2022)

The City of Campbelltown, part of the state of New South Wales in Australia, developed a communications plan to provide clarity and improve consistency in its approach to internal and external communications processes and practices. As part of its strategic approach, the plan maps short, medium and long-term goals, together with concrete indicators to measure performance. It also has a matrix system that allows for the monitoring of progress with clear information on:

- Objective
- Concrete action
- Level of priority
- Responsible Officer
- Budget Requirement
- Timeframe

The plan was developed to leverage synergies with the locality's broader strategic planning framework, as it brings together the Revised Strategic Plan 'Towards 2020', its Corporate Style Guide and Digital Media Strategy.

Source: Campbelltown City Council (2017), Communications Management Plan 2017-2022, available online at: https://www.campbelltown.sa.gov.au/webdata/resources/files/Communications%20Plan.pdf

The Government of Jersey's Communications Strategy and Plan (2019)

The 2019 Government Communications Strategy and Plan is a formal document that sets out the purpose, role and strategic objectives of communications for the Government of Jersey. It details the activities that we be collectively undertaken by all departments in delivering the wide range of day-to-day public services. It supports the promotion of policy, the transparency of performance, and the range of internal activities that underpin public services, such as Finance, procurement, HR and IT, and the two-way communication and engagement with 100,000 islanders and 6,700 public servants.

The strategy identifies six strategic objectives for communications. It summarises the priorities for action to transform communications into a modern, professional operation. It maps different internal and external audiences, while setting channels for each activity. The strategy also includes a communication plan that provides details at a more granular level. It also details the professional principles and standards.

Source: Government of Jersey (2019), Communications Strategy and Plan 2019, available online at: https://www.gov.je/SiteCollectionDocuments/Government%20and%20administration/ID%20Comms%20Strategy%20and%20Plan%20190222%20CC.pdf

In Jordan, local authorities interact regularly with citizens as part of the process to collect needs, but analysis suggests that public communication activities are done on an ad hoc and informal basis. While 69% of the respondents to the OECD survey noted that their office has a communication plan, interviews revealed that these are often not formalized or widely distributed. Developing a written planning document by each sub-national authority could support the setting of a structured communication approach and establish the direction of initiatives, together with short, medium and long-term goals. A written plan could also provide a clear framework for communication activities to be monitored and evaluated, to ensure that initiatives reach their desired objectives.

To support the creation and implementation of sub-national plans, a national roadmap or strategy on communicating the Decentralization Reform in Jordan could also be developed as a framework for local communicators. In this regard, the Ministry of Local Affairs together with the Ministry of State for Media Affairs – the institution in charge of steering whole-of-government communications in Jordan - could guide such an endeavour.

For a plan to be implemented effectively, however, local authorities will need to establish formal communication structures, modernize communication capacities and address the uneven levels of skills across and within Governorates. During OECD interviews, civil servants noted the lack of or insufficient human resources and competencies as one of the most pressing challenges in building awareness on local participation opportunities. It was also noted that communication guidelines for local actors are inexistent.

The effective engagement of citizens in the needs assessment process will thus require the hiring and training of dedicated communication staff with qualified and diverse profiles, in particular within Municipal Local Development Units (LDUs) and Governorate Development Units (GDUs). Capacity building efforts could focus on developing relevant skills, such as social media use, communicating with youth, monitoring and evaluation and responding to online disinformation. The government of Canada, for example, provides a series of monthly capacity building events to local communicators (see Box 3.2).

Box 3.2. Canada's Communications Community Office efforts to build communication skills across the public sector

The Communications Community Office (CCO) in Canada provides support to communications professionals with the aim to enhance their skills and build communities of practice. The office provides a variety of services, including regular learning events, access to the latest communications news and information. Its Steering Committee is made up of Directors, Directors General (DGs) and Assistant Deputy Ministers (ADMs) of Communications, providing direction and setting priority areas for capacity building across regions in Canada.

As part of its mandate, the CCO conducts capacity building workshops for public communicators, both in person and via MOOCS, webcast or WebEx. Often, these events focus on an expert sharing their knowledge and lessons learned about a new approach, tool or challenge, ensuring that knowledge is shared within government. In 2018, the CCO organized a series of monthly workshops on relevant subjects such as:

- Communicating with Millenials
- Developing high-impact social media campaigns
- Journey Mapping
- The Power of Plain Language
- Speechwriting
- Opioids Crisis: Why Words Matter
- How Communicators Contribute to Web Success
- Words Matter: An Indigenous Glossary of Terms
- Planning Inclusive and Accessible Events
- Public Opinion Research in Government
- Chatbots –Get to know this smart solution

In addition, a key event organized by the CCO is the annual Learning Day, which in 2018 brought together over 700 communicators across the country to learn, share and network.

Source: Government of Canada (2019), Communications Community Office 2018-2019 Annual Report, available online at: https://www.canada.ca/en/privy-council/services/communications-community-office/reports/annual-2018-2019-fiscal-year.html

---

As mentioned in Chapter 2, the lack of clarity of roles and responsibilities has also presented important barriers to information sharing and coordination, including those regarding communication initiatives within each Governorate. The interviews conducted by the OECD highlighted that coordination tends to vary significantly across regions, as the sharing of information (i.e. on participation activities and the list of needs more generally) between Local, Municipal and Governorate Councils, is done informally. The alignment of messages and activities throughout the stages of the needs assessment, both horizontally and vertically across levels of government, is critical to maximise their impact.

In this context, the biggest challenges exist between Municipal and Governorate levels. During validation workshops, government representatives from all levels agreed on the need to increase the coordination of communication initiatives. In each Governorate, regular meetings of the Executive Committee take place every two weeks, but neither records nor an information repository is kept or shared. In this regard, making use of online platforms could help align activities and identify potential synergies between municipal and governorate actors. Indeed, isolated efforts may reduce the impact and awareness of messages and increase the risk of sharing contradictory information.

Consequently, GDUs in coordination with LDUs, could strengthen their roles as the co-ordinating actors of communication activities at the level of each Governorate. By centralizing the coordination role, these actors could organize regular meetings with staff in charge of communications from different municipalities to ensure that activities around the needs assessment process are disseminated effectively. In the UK, for instance, a local government association was created to coordinate consistent and impactful campaigns (see Box 3.3). In addition, the use of online coordination tools, such as Trello or other online scheduling tools, could help map ongoing activities and ensure that the messages are aligned.

Box 3.3. The Local Government Association in the United Kingdom

In the United Kingdom, the Local Government Association (LGA) brings together the institutions of local government across the country to support, promote and improve service delivery at a council level. One of the priorities of the LGA involves securing long-term funding for local government.

The LGA therefore launched a campaign called #CouncilsCan to advocate for long-term investment in local government and secure a share of government spending reviews for local governments. The LGA uses the campaign to demonstrate the positive impact of the services its members provide to their communities and to encourage the national government to provide local councils with certainty about their future income. To do so, the campaign uses a range of communications materials to raise awareness and advocate for its cause. To engage local communities and encourage them to back the campaign, for example, the #CouncilsCan campaign includes a focus on *'unsung heroes'*, i.e. council workers who work hard to improve lives in their communities such as library staff, health visitors, school nurses, streetcleaners and disability welfare officers. Such stories personalise the work of local administrations and encourage greater support from residents whose lives may have been touched by such employees. The LGA has also organised debates with parliamentarians to raise awareness of the issues and encourage discussion of the need to prioritise council funding.

The campaign has delivered success for the LGA, with Government Spending Reviews beginning to increase the certainty for local councils about their budgets, including committed funding for social care and support for children and young people with special educational needs.

Source: Local Government Association (N.D), About and Campaigns websites, available online at: https://www.local.gov.uk/about & https://www.local.gov.uk/about/campaigns/councilscan

Strengthening implementation efforts around the Access to Information (ATI) right at the subnational level

Ensuring access to relevant and clear information are key pillars of an open government. The OECD defines access to information (ATI) as "an initial level of participation characterized by a one-way relationship in which the government produces and delivers information to stakeholders" (OECD, 2016). It covers both its provision on demand (i.e. ATI requests) as well as proactive disclosure measures by government entities.

The proactive disclosure of information allows citizens to gain a better understanding of issues that matter most to them (OECD, 2019a). Its proactive sharing not only ensures transparency around the policy making process, but it enables citizens to participate effectively throughout all its stages. As a common practice in most OECD countries, local authorities often publish documents such as (OECD, 2019b):

* Information on the activities of public authorities;
* Information on the finances of public authorities (i.e. annual budget, annual budget of previous years, annual financial reports);

- Public authorities' news and events;
- Calendar of activities and meetings;
- Information on public consultations;
- Information on public tenders and contracts for public service;
- Information on partnerships (i.e. with businesses, local influencers, etc);
- Information on training opportunities;
- Awareness raising on specific thematic policy areas; and
- Information on anti-corruption policies and activities.

In terms of ATI, Jordan was the first country in the MENA region to adopt a law in this regard in 2007. However, this right remains under-utilised by citizens and capacity gaps to implement this law exist across the public service (OECD, 2019c). In fact, only 10,305 requests were filed by citizens between 2012 and 2015 and amounted to 12,101 in 2016 (Ibid). Findings from OECD validation meetings noted that these challenges are exacerbated at the subnational level, where procedures to address information requests remain unclear, in particular at the level of municipalities.

As a first step to ensuring an effective communication, the Jordanian Government should promote the proactive organization and publishing of information. Findings from OECD validation workshops yielded that citizens struggle to find relevant information, such as the final local development plan and list of approved needs. To this end, it will be critical to make available in an easy, clear and understandable format basic information on the decentralization reform. The use of clear language would also allow citizens to more easily understand their role, in particular the steps of how needs and budget priorities are identified and set, the responsibilities of Municipal and Governorate Councils, and the opportunities for them to participate. The City of Barrie in Canada, for example, publishes meeting calendars, summary records and material on local policies on a regular basis in their main webpage to facilitate the sharing and access to local public information (see Box 3.4).

The City of Barrie, in the State of Ontario Canada, developed a systematic approach for City Council and other local committees to communicate with citizens and vice versa.

Citizens are able to communicate and engage with the local council and committees through institutionalized formal and informal channels. Formal communication channels are a matter of public record, and are documented and referred to throughout Council's decision-making process. These channels include the use of circulation lists, open delegations, public meetings and open presentations and deputations. In addition, the city council made available a guide to communicating with city council outlining each of the steps and procedures for citizens to engage. In addition, informal communication channels, such as correspondence, neighbourhood meetings and town hall meetings, are set in place to adjust to different audience needs.

The Barrie city council has also opened channels for citizens to access relevant and timeline information on city council sessions. Through the city's portal, citizens are able to access in real time an up to date calendar of meetings for City Council, General Committee and all Reference Committees. The calendar (http://barrie.legistar.com/Calendar.aspx) includes documents on meeting details, agenda, minutes and video recording of the session.

Source: City of Barrie, Canada (N.D), The City of Barrie portal, accessed online on 4 September 2019, https://www.barrie.ca/City%20Hall/MayorCouncil/Council%20Committees/Pages/default.aspx

In parallel, the effective implementation of the ATI right will require addressing the capacity gaps of sub-national authorities to respond to information requests. In line with OECD practices, a first step to support the implementation of the ATI law will require awareness raising around this right, as well as on the necessary procedures and protocols for local public servants to follow (see Box 3.5 for an example of a board game used in Mexico for this purpose). In this regard the leading implementers of the ATI commitment in Jordan's 4th OGP national action plan (NAP) – namely the Department of the National Library, the Ministry of Information and Communications Technology, and the Integrity and Anti - Corruption Commission - could play an important role leading implementation efforts around this law at the sub-national level.

To help answer questions related to Mexico's ATI law, Article 19 in Mexico City created a board game called "Your right to know", with the aim to help civil society, journalists and activists learn how to use ATI laws to guarantee their rights, acquire knowledge and hold governments and institutions to account. It has been highly successful in Mexico City and disseminated by the Mexican National Institute for Transparency, Access to Information and Personal Data Protection (INAI). The game covers practical modules on how to create and submit a request, relevant institutions involved in the process, the types of public information that exist and the processes for appeals.

Source: Article 19 Mexico City (2019), «Tu derecho a saber» un juego para aprender cómo funciona el derecho a la información, https://www.article19.org/wp-content/uploads/2019/09/FOI-snakes-and-ladders-Spanish-Final_compressed.pdf

To increase the visibility and momentum around the promotion of this right, the Government of Jordan could consider expanding the scope of ATI commitments as part of the country's open government agenda to explicitly target local actors. Notably, there is an immediate opportunity to include local stakeholders in activities from commitment 5 of Jordan's 4th OGP NAP (2018 – 2020), and even greater chances to concretely target these actors in Jordan's forthcoming 5th OGP NAP. Efforts in the framework of OGP activities led by the Open Government Unit in MoPIC currently focus on the institutionalization of the enforcement measures for the ATI Law with activities around awareness raising, building capacities and monitoring progress. Indeed, equipping local actors with the knowledge and skills to guarantee this right is all the more important in the context of decentralizing the design of local policies and services.

Promoting the proactive disclosure of relevant, clear and timely information on the process and results of collecting needs

Strengthening transparency at the local level will require authorities to use public communication as a tool to systematically raise citizens' awareness on decentralization activities and results. In Jordan, only 10% of the population feel informed about the decentralization process, while 57% remain unaware of the new roles of Governorate and Municipal Councils in the design and implementation of Governorate Development Plans (International Republican Institute, 2018). These findings align with OECD survey data, where a majority of sub-national authorities (63%) signalled the lack of awareness of civil society as a pressing challenge for their inclusion in the needs assessment process (See Figure 3.2 and Figure 3.3).

Figure 3.2. Lack of awareness as one of the main issues to engage stakeholders in the needs assessment process

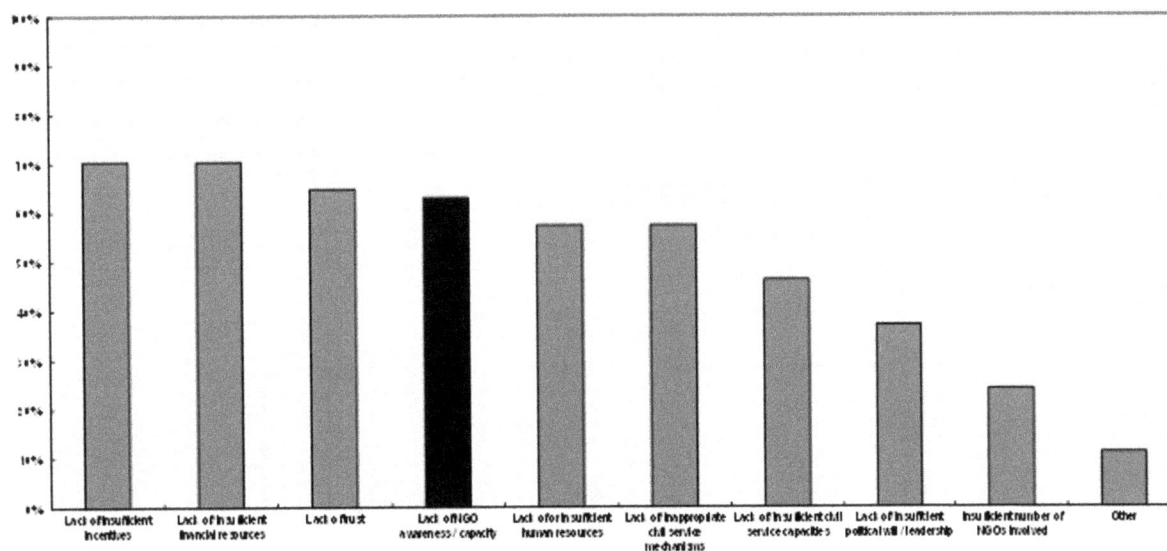

Source: OECD (2019) Questionnaire for sub-national governments: Stakeholder participation in Jordan's needs assessment process.

Figure 3.3. Share of sub-national authorities selecting lack of awareness of NGOs on opportunities for engagement as a key challenge for their inclusion in the needs assessment process

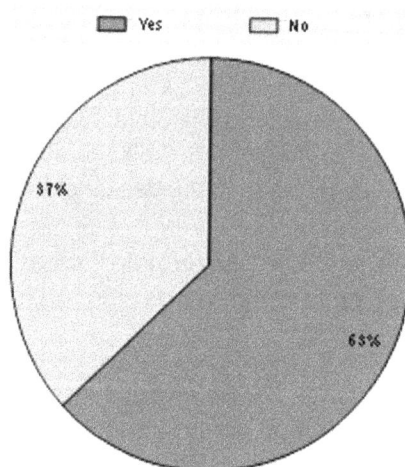

Source: OECD (2019) Questionnaire for sub-national governments: Stakeholder participation in Jordan's needs assessment process.

Strengthening citizen participation in the design of local development plans will thus require the provision of timely and relevant information on the entire needs assessment process, including the criteria for selection of budget priorities. Notably, OECD data shows that a majority of NGOs (77%) were not aware of the criteria used to define priorities for local investments in 2018. An even greater share (83%) were not aware of the results communicated by public authorities, and only 10% were informed as to why some needs were or were not funded in 2018 (see Figure 3.4). Thus, the lack of information on the process and its results risks exacerbating general feelings of scepticisms and distrust, which in turn can contribute to growing disengagement levels. To address this challenge, sub-national authorities could consider proactively sharing information regarding the criteria for the allocation of budget priorities, the final list of financed projects and the justification for their selection.

Figure 3.4. Share of NGOs aware of the criteria for project selection, the final results and their justification

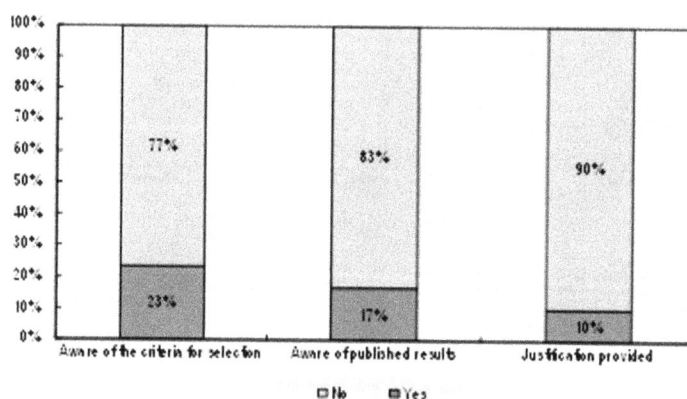

Source: OECD (2019) Questionnaire for Civil Society Organizations: Stakeholder participation in Jordan's needs assessment process.

In addition, representatives from Governorate offices noted during validation workshops that citizens struggle to identify priority needs to be translated to local development projects, and often put forward those that are not relevant for the level of government at which they are engaging. For example, needs collected in 2018 were primarily focused on health, education and public roads, which are services that are not provided by municipalities (Khadim, 2018). Therefore, publishing the metrics used for the selection of budget priorities would not only make the selection process more transparent, but it could also increase the relevance of citizens' contributions.

Finally, while direct communication with the public is a key lever to raising awareness, the media remains an important intermediary and represent an essential element of a democratic society. Journalists can transmit and analyse information, as well as hold the government to account and represent the voices of citizens (OECD, 2019a). Recognizing the media as a partner allows for public communicators to reach a wider audience and strategically disseminate targeted messages. Therefore, the promotion of the active participation of the media in the needs assessment process could help build support around its activities.

Developing a more sophisticated use of communication channels according to the needs and preferences of different audiences

Understanding audiences and the behavioural context is a key element of an effective two-way communication approach. Notably, gathering and using audience insights can aid in the delivery of personalized communications to different segments of the population that reflect their diverse needs, perceptions, fears and habits.

Indeed, promoting an open dialogue with citizens requires authorities to understand the needs and media consumption patterns from different audiences to select the appropriate mix of channels for engagement. In terms of information sharing, OECD survey results indicate a clear preference by local authorities to use social media (72%) and formal communication (62%), including the use of official government letters (See Figure 3.5). Interestingly, there is a steep disparity between the use of popular channels and the more traditional ones, such as government websites, TV and Radio. This can be attributed in part to the potential to reduce costs and the current media landscape in Jordan, which has made social media channels more attractive as most news outlets are concentrated in Amman.

Figure 3.5. Channels used by sub-national authorities in Jordan to inform the public about needs assessment activities and encourage participation

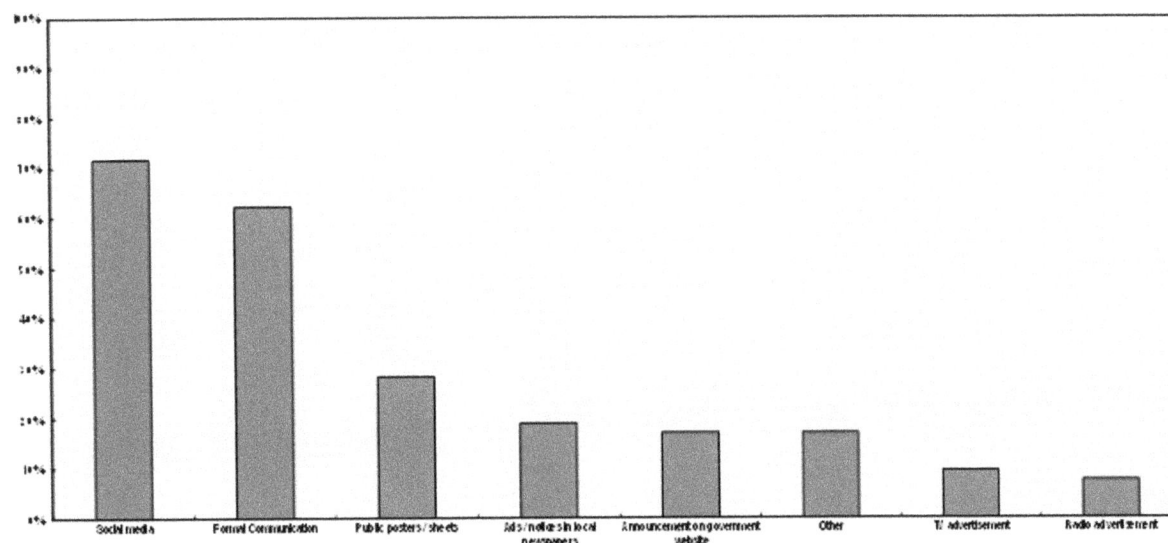

Source: OECD (2019) Questionnaire for sub-national governments: Stakeholder participation in Jordan's needs assessment process.

Interestingly, citizens generally agree that online communication channels, including social media platforms, are the most effective means for engagement. OECD survey results revealed that social media (73%), emails (43%) and phone calls (43%) were the top three channels selected by CSOs as the most effective means to communicate with sub-national authorities (see Figure 3.6). Moreover, a study by Northwestern University (2017) found that smartphones (77%) are the second preferred means for Jordanians to consult news. Facebook is also becoming an increasingly important source of information, with almost half of the population (41%) making use of this platform for such a purpose.

Figure 3.6. Channels considered as the top three most effective means of communication with local and municipal government representatives in Jordan

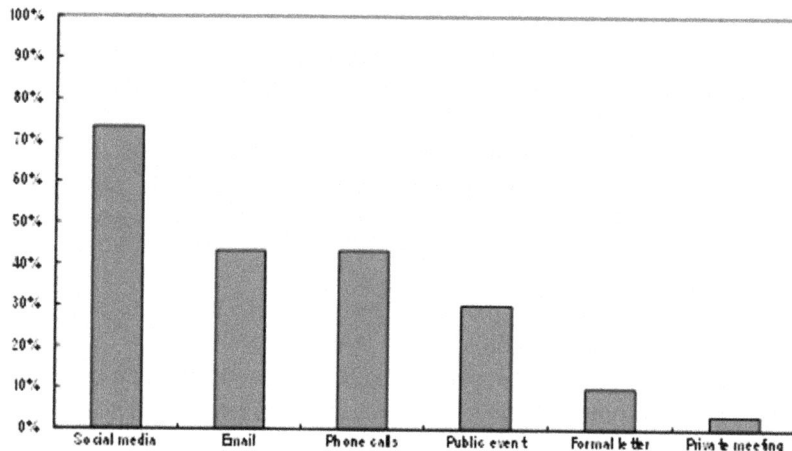

Source: OECD (2019) Questionnaire for Civil Society Organizations: Stakeholder participation in Jordan's needs assessment process.

Where possible, local authorities should make use of data on news consumption trends to tailor their selection of audiences and channels. While social media can be an effective means to communicate, care must be taken in terms of channel selection to ensure that vulnerable segments of the population can also access relevant information, in particular as internet access and digital literacy levels vary significantly across governorates. The State of Victoria in Australia, for example, uses a multi-channel strategy based on the needs of different audiences to consult them on major infrastructure project decisions (see Box 3.6).

Box 3.6. Communicating with local communities in Victoria on the Level Crossing Removal Programme

The Australian State of Victoria created the Level Crossing Removal Authority to manage one of the state's biggest ever rail infrastructure projects, notably the elimination of 75 level crossing across the city of Melbourne. The project also involved general improvements to the rail network. The goal of the project was to improve public safety, reduce congestion, improve the reliability of travel services and to increase network capacity.

The Victorian government recognised that it would be important that the local community was consulted and kept informed about the progress of the work. To this end, a dedicated website and associated materials such as a newsletter and social media channels were created to provide updates on the scheme. These updates included news about which areas of the city are likely to experience disruption as works are carried out. The communication platform also includes a feedback mechanism which enables residents to engage with a customer service team, who are able to answer questions and offer advice. The website also asks for input as the project develops. For example, local businesses are asked for their opinion about the design and planning and process and thoughts on how the area can be redeveloped as a result of the level crossing removal.

Regular progress updates are provided so that residents can clearly understand why work is being carried out, the timeline for completion, and the future plans for the area. For each area, a FAQ is provided with clear information, while fact sheets can also be downloaded, as well as the designs for the project. Residents can ask questions via a public forum, which are answered by the project team. They can also share ideas they may have about what they would like to see in the area as part of its redevelopment such as green spaces or cafes. The websites are highly visual and creative in design. Videos bring the project to life, while interactive maps enable clear visualisation of progress.

Overall, the communications campaign around the Level Crossing Removal programme has helped to make the process smoother and win greater support and engagement from local communities.

Source: Author's own work based on : https://levelcrossings.vic.gov.au/about

As local authorities increasingly turn to social media, these actors could benefit from using online platforms in a more strategic way. There is an opportunity at hand to leverage the immediate, interactive and cost-saving benefits of these platforms, given that more than half of the population actively using WhatsApp (78%), Facebook (70%) and YouTube (49%) (Northwestern University, 2018). However, the OECD found that even though 72% of sub-national authorities had a presence on social media, low levels of engagement and trust remain due to generic posts and insufficient engagement with public comments. Building on the active posting of information on Facebook and Twitter, such as the Municipality of Salt, local authorities could also collect citizen feedback, for instance, during the process of collecting needs and communicating the final selected list of priorities. For example, the City of Vancouver made use of social media to develop its new transportation policy through the use of e-deliberation practices (See Box 3.7).

Box 3.7. E-deliberation on Facebook: The City of Vancouver's Transportation Policy

In 2011, over 500 residents of the City of Vancouver participated in "Exploring Vancouver's Transportation Future" through an e-deliberative process on Facebook. This Facebook event was one of a number of engagement mechanisms used by the government to develop the city's transportation policy; activities also included in-person workshops, presentations, paper and online surveys, and an online discussion forum.

During the first phase of the process, twelve Facebook groups were created with 45 participants each, according to their commuting habits and demographic characteristics. Participants then engaged in discussions, led by a facilitator, for over two and half weeks on key issues related to transportation – such as health, affordability, economy, and the environment. Each group then proposed a series of recommendations for the City's Transportation Plan and voted on their three favourite ones.

All proposals from each of the 12 groups were streamlined into a document with 19 recommendations for Vancouver's transportation plan. Among these recommendations, seven ideas emerged on cycling, five on public transit, three on land use, two on public space, and two on pedestrian walkways. The recommendations were discussed publicly on Facebook for ten days in late June 2011.

Resulting from the extensive process of online consultation, the City of Vancouver Transportation 2040 team wrote a four page response to each of the nineteen recommendations with concrete initiatives or plans.

Source: Haas, S. (2012), Exploring Facebook's potential for deliberative public engagement on sustainable policy, https://pics.uvic.ca/sites/default/files/uploads/publications/HaasLyons_Thesis.pdf

---

However, without a tailored strategy or guidelines, local governments' use of social media will not harness its full potential. Rather, solely sharing information through online platforms may have the adverse effect of disengaging citizens through seemingly unresponsive communication. Recognizing the potential of social media to promote civic participation, sub-national authorities, with the support of MoSMA and MoLA, could prioritize the development of a shared set of guidelines and consider the inclusion of specific objectives and indicators within communication plans.

In addition to choosing the right channels, tailoring messages to the context of local stakeholders through the understanding of different audiences can be an additional element of an effective communication. This is particularly important in Jordan, considering the growing fragmentation and diversity of audiences across and within each of the 12 Governorates.

In Jordan, with close to 70% of the population below the age 30, messages should be differentiated to reflect these demographic factors (OECD, 2018). In this regard, a particular focus should be given to learning more about youth audiences, adapting communications to their preferred means for engagement and exploring opportunities to promote their participation in the needs assessment process. Special attention could be payed to opening spaces for online participation on social media, as the most used platforms by young people (ages 18-22) in Jordan include WhatsApp (82%), Facebook (82%) YouTube (63%) and Instagram (57%) respectively (Northwestern University, 2018). In return, tailoring communication for young people would not only increase the responsiveness of policies and services, but could also promote their engagement in the wider decentralization process. The OECD developed a guide with concrete principles to promote a meaningful communication with youth (see Box 3.8).

Box 3.8. The OECD Engaging Young People in Open Government Communication Guide

The OECD "Engaging young people in open government" communication guide is provides public communicators with ideas and approaches on how to effectively communicate with youth in order to promote their participation, drawing on recent research and case studies from across OECD member and partner countries. It highlights the benefits of engaging young people in public life to harness the demographic dividend, encourage innovation and economic development, build an active citizenship and help shape the online debate. It provides concrete avenues for communicators to learn more about youth audiences, reach them effectively and ultimately promote their participation in the design and delivery of policies and services.

Source: OECD (2019), Engaging young people in open government: a communication guide, Paris publishing, https://www.oecd.org/mena/governance/Young-people-in-OG.pdf

In parallel, highlighting messages that reflect specific regional and demographic concerns (i.e. gender sensitive communication, age trends, etc.) could in turn increase participation levels in the needs assessment process. In particular, close attention should be payed to communication with vulnerable segments of the population. To this end, it will be important to ensure a mapping of audiences, potentially by GDUs and LDUs jointly, to tailor messages and channels to the specific needs of each community.

Recommendations

Public communication can be a valuable tool supporting the needs assessment process at the sub-national level in Jordan. To reap its full benefits, efforts should focus on developing a more strategic approach to communicating with citizens by formalizing actions through strategies and plans, coordinating initiatives and addressing current capacity gaps. Ensuring greater transparency and access to up–to-date, clear and relevant information will also be important to enable the participation of citizens in the process to collect local needs. In addition, there is an opportunity for local authorities to develop a more sophisticated use of communications according to the needs and preferences of different audiences.

To this end, the Government of Jordan could adopt the following recommendations:

- Sub-national authorities could develop, on their own or jointly, a written communication plan to institutionalize communication activities. Such plans would facilitate more effective communications, as well as build awareness and buy-in efforts within government. The plans would also assist the monitoring and evaluation of communication activities to ensure they achieve their desired impact. These plans should be based on audience insights. Ultimately, formal plans should aim to promote the active participation of civil society, private sector, the media and the public at large.
- Develop a national communications strategy for the decentralization process, to clarify how to inform citizens of the available opportunities for participation, the overall process of the needs assessment, its progress and impact achieved. A national strategy outlining the overall vision of decentralization could serve as the basis for each governorate to develop their own communication plans. The Ministry of Local Affairs together with the Ministry of State for Media Affairs could guide such an endeavour, together with other relevant line ministries in Jordan.
- Build the capacities of local civil servants to ensure they have the skills to communicate effectively with stakeholders throughout the phases of the needs assessment process (i.e. data analytics, social media use and online participation methods, etc.). In this regard, MoLA could coordinate with the Ministry of State for Media Affairs to develop a communication manual or a set of

guidelines. These tools would help standardize procedures, clarify roles and promote a more coordinated approach between the three levels of government.

- Coordinate messages and communication activities between local and governorate levels. Make use of new digital platforms – such as Trello, Slack and WhatsApp – to facilitate internal communication between government stakeholders from local, municipal and governorate levels.

- Local Development Councils could strengthen their role as co-ordinating actors of public communication activities at the local level.

- In regards to ATI, Jordan should continue its efforts to support the effective implementation of this right in coordination with the Open Government Unit in MoPIC. Measures should clarify the rules and procedures around how public institutions categorize and share information, as well as the information flows with citizens. Efforts could also promote the proactive disclosure the needs assessment results and the approved list. This could be done through coordination with the National Library to increase the quality and frequency of data shared with the public. To increase visibility and momentum around the promotion of this right, the Government could also consider expanding the scope of existing ATI commitments in the country's open government agenda to explicitly target local actors.

- Governorates could clarify and publish the criteria for selection of budget priorities from the early stages of the needs cycle.

- Improve the feedback process and clarify why needs were or were not selected. This would facilitate the process of communicating results and impact to citizens, which in turn could help raise awareness and buy-in regarding the decentralization process.

- Subnational authorities should considering using a diverse range of communication channels to reach a variety of stakeholders based on audience insights to reflect different needs and media consumption patterns. To this end, an initial mapping of audiences could be conducted, potentially by GDUs and LDUs jointly, to tailor messages and channels to the specific needs of each community.

- As sub-national authorities are increasingly adopting social media to communicate with citizens, it will be important to ensure the existence of social media guidelines, capacity building of public communicators and the adoption of new and relevant skills to match users' needs. These initiatives could be coordinated with the support of MoLA and MoSMA.

- Ensure that communication is tailored to the needs of different segments of the population, based on demographic factors and regional needs. I particular, subnational authorities should pay special attention to sharing information with vulnerable segments of the population.

- Tailoring communication for young people would not only increase the responsiveness of policies and services, but could also promote their engagement in the wider decentralization and policy-making processes. Subnational authorities could consider developing a specific engagement plan with youth, making use of social media platforms, to increase their participation in the design and delivery of local development plans.

References

Gobierno de Chile (N.D.), *Kit Digital*, accessed on 15 May 2019, http://kitdigital.gob.cl/

Graham, M. (2014), *Government communication in the digital age: Social media's effect on local government public relations*, Public Relations Inquiry Journal, volume 3, n°3, septembre, https://doi.org/10.1177/2046147X14545371.

Institute for Strategic Dialogue (2014), *Countering the appeal of online extremism, Policy Brief,* available online at:

https://www.dhs.gov/sites/default/files/publications/Countering%20the%20Appeal%20of%20Extremis m%20Online-ISD%20Report.pdf

International Republican Institute (2018), *Public Opinion Survey: Residents of Jordan*, Center for Insights in Survey Research, available online at: https://www.iri.org/resource/jordan-poll-reveals-low-trust-government-increasing-economic-hardship

Kadhim, M. (2018), *Political Economy Analysis of Jordan*, developed within the framework of the USAID project Cities Implementing Transparent, Innovative and Effective Solutions (CITIES).

Mahadin E., Binda C. & Khasawneh M. (2018), *Legal Review of the Jordanian Decentralization Law*, issued by Karak Castle Center for Consultations and Training.

Murphy, K. (2019), *Government Communications in a Digital Age: A Comparative Study of Online Government Communications in Germany and Great Britain*, ISBN 978-3-8487-5658-2.

North Western University (2018), *Media Use in the Middle East*, Qatar, available online at: http://www.mideastmedia.org/survey/2018/interactive/online-and-social-media/who-use-the-following-social-media-platforms.html#Q6%5B%5D=%3D1&Q4%5B%5D=BETWEEN+18+AND+24

NorthWestern University in Qatar (2017), *Media Use in the Middle* East, Qatar, http://www.mideastmedia.org/survey/2017/interactive/social-media/who-use-the-following-social-media-platforms-facebook-whatsapp-twitter-instagram-snapchat-youtube-etc.html

OECD (2019a), *Voix citoyenne au Maroc: Le rôle de la communication et des médias pour un gouvernement plus ouvert*, Examens de l'OCDE sur la gouvernance publique, OECD Publishing, Paris, https://doi.org/10.1787/9789264306608-fr.

OECD (2019b), *Open Government in Tunisia: La Marsa, Sayada and Sfax*, OECD Public Governance Reviews, OECD Publishing, Paris, https://doi.org/10.1787/9789264310995-en.

OECD (2019c), Institutions Guaranteeing Access to Information: OECD and MENA Region, OECD Publishing, Paris, https://doi.org/10.1787/e6d58b52-en.

OECD Development Centre (2018), *Youth Well-being Policy Review of Jordan*, EU-OECD Youth Inclusion Project, Paris.

OECD (2017a), *The OECD Recommendation of the Council on Open Government*, OECD Legal Instruments, Paris, https://legalinstruments.oecd.org/public/doc/359/d5392da9-6aa6-4647-b266-2e37694c497f.htm

OECD (2017b), *Contextualising decentralisation reform and open government in Jordan*, in Towards a New Partnership with Citizens: Jordan's Decentralisation Reform, OECD Publishing, Paris, https://doi.org/10.1787/9789264275461-5-en.

OECD (2017c), *Organisation and functions at the centre of government: Centre Stage II*, survey response report, internal document.

OECD (2016), *Open Government: The Global Context and the Way Forward*, OECD Publishing, Paris, https://doi.org/10.1787/9789264268104-en.

UNDP & UNICEF (2015), *Socio-economic Inequality in Jordan*, online publication available at: https://www.undp.org/content/dam/jordan/docs/Poverty/UNDP%20Socio%20economic%20Inequality %20in%20Jordan%20English.pdf

Chapter 4. Stakeholder Participation in the Needs Assessment Process

This chapter highlights the opportunities to embed stakeholder participation at the local level in Jordan. It analyses current efforts from sub-national authorities to better inform, consult and engage stakeholders across the needs assessment process. It also identifies a number of implications that need to be tackled to successfully grasp the potential benefits of stakeholder participation in Jordan.

With the adoption of the 2015 Municipalities and Decentralization laws in Jordan, the Government has set a priority to empower local communities in the definition of policy and budgetary priorities across the 12 Governorates. Notably, the creation of Elected Councils has advanced efforts to bring public institutions closer to the public. More importantly, the reform has furthered the opening of the government by placing citizens at the heart of policies and services through a bottom-up approach to develop local plans.

Indeed, stakeholder participation allows governments to bridge the divide with citizens, and is at the core of responsive policy-making and service delivery. The OECD defines stakeholder participation as "all the ways in which stakeholders can be involved in the policy cycle and in service design and delivery (OECD, 2017a)." The OECD Recommendation of the Council on Open Government (2017), furthermore, argues that granting all stakeholders equal and fair opportunities to be engaged are key elements of effective open government reforms.

As part of its framework of analysis, the OECD ladder of participation model distinguishes between three levels of stakeholder participation, namely information, consultation and engagement (OECD, 2017):

- Information: refers to the one-way relationship in which public organisations produce and share information for the general public, which cover both "reactive" measures responding to citizens' information demands and "proactive" measures to disclose information and publish open data sets.
- Consultation: refers to the two-way relationship in which citizens provide feedback to the government, where public institutions still define the issues for consultation, set the questions and manage the consultative process.
- Engagement: refers to the provision of opportunities for stakeholders, as well as adequate resources (e.g. information, data and digital tools), to collaborate with public institutions throughout the policy-making cycle (OECD, 2016). It may include elements of co-decision or co-production.

Embedding stakeholder participation in the way local policies and services are designed in Jordan is all the more important against a backdrop of declining trust in public institutions. In fact, levels of trust in government are at their lowest, having suffered a steep decline from 73% in 2011 to 38% in 2018 (Arab Barometer, 2019). As noted in Chapter 3, a perception survey identified that only 10% of the population feel informed about the decentralization process, while 57% remain unaware of the new roles of Governorate and Municipal Councils and available opportunities to participate in the needs assessment process (International Republic Institute, 2018). OECD interviews with representatives from local government and civil society organizations (CSOs) also highlight room for improvement to increase opportunities for engagement and awareness raising.

The following chapter therefore provides an assessment of and recommendations for Jordan to embed stakeholder participation in the needs assessment process effectively. It examines the impact of current practices of Local, Municipal and Governorate authorities to consult and engage stakeholders in the needs assessment process.

Embedding stakeholder participation at the local level in Jordan

As the requirements on local governments to implement the decentralization reforms increase, so does the imperative to bridge the divide with citizens. In this respect, embedding participation at the local level acts as a virtuous circle by involving the public more deeply in policy choices and thereby reinforcing trust (OECD, 2016). Broadly, the aim of the decentralization reform in Jordan is to expand engagement efforts with citizens through the needs cycle, showcase impact, help ensure development plans reflect community needs more accurately and ultimately build trust.

Similar to most OECD countries, there is a stark difference between trust at the national and local level in Jordan, where citizens have greater confidence in Municipal Governments (52%) and Governorate

Councils (44%) than in the Parliament (13%)[1] (International Republican Institute, 2018). Indeed, the relatively higher levels of trust at the sub-national level in Jordan present an opportunity to engage actively with communities, and in turn contribute to better public services.

While trust levels at the local level remain higher than those at the national level, there remains, however, room for improvement. According to OECD data, the majority of public officials (65%) identified the lack of trust between the government and citizens as a challenge to increasing their involvement in the needs assessment process. Interestingly, the "lack of trust between government, citizens and CSOs" was also the top challenge selected by civil society (70%) (see Figure 4.1).

Figure 4.1. Percentage of sub-national authorities and CSOs selecting "lack of trust" as a key challenge in the needs assessment process

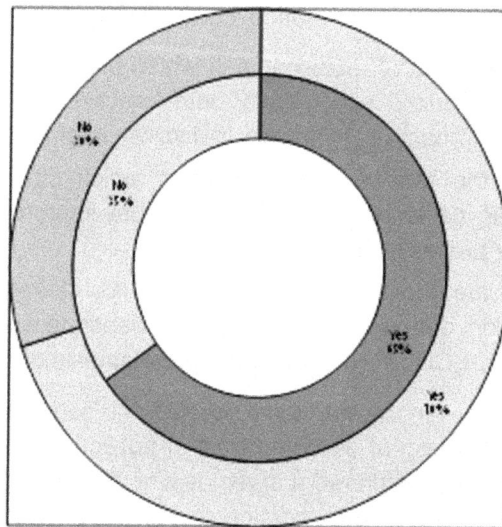

Note: The inner circle reflects the responses from sub-national authorities and the outer circle those from CSOs.
Source: OECD (2019) Questionnaire for Civil Society Organizations & sub-national authorities: Stakeholder participation in Jordan's needs assessment process.

In addition, scepticism remains among some CSOs as to whether local development plans will meet citizens' needs and expectations. A majority of civil society responding to the OECD survey emphasized the lack of trust (70%) and motivation (60%) as the main drivers of low participation in the collection of needs (See Figure 4.2). In particular, concerns remain in regards to the highly bureaucratic nature of this bottom-up process and the need to still rely on informal relationships to advocate for specific initiatives (Mahadin et al., 2018). Indeed, implementation efforts around the decentralization reform have brought to light the need for local authorities to establish a meaningful partnership with citizens, civil society and the private sector.

Figure 4.2. Main challenges to engage stakeholders in the needs assessment process

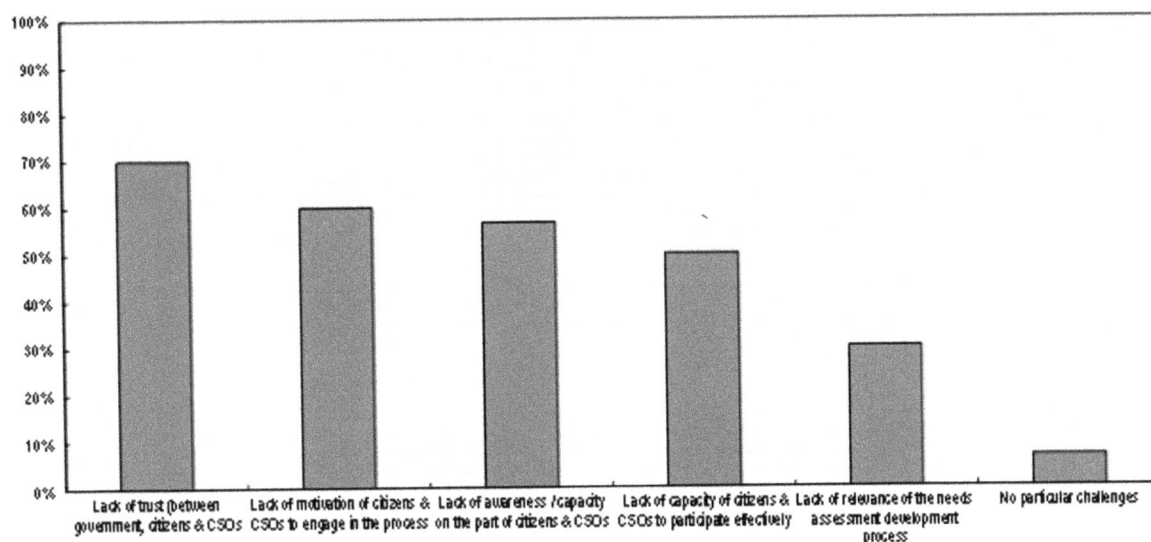

Source: OECD (2019), Questionnaire for Civil Society: Stakeholder participation in Jordan's needs assessment process.

Recognizing these challenges, the Jordanian Government is also prioritizing stakeholder participation at the local level, acknowledging it as an important pillar of its national vision. One of the objectives of the Government Renaissance Plan (2019 – 2020), for example, is to promote the participation of local communities to identify development priorities and ensure their positive reflection on the quality of public services. The Renaissance Plan also recognizes the need to systematically integrate youth in this process. In addition to the 2015 Decentralization laws, commitments toward promoting the engagement of stakeholders as part of this reform were also undertaken through Jordan's 3rd and 4th OGP NAPs.

In efforts to take stock and discuss the country's progress, the Government also conducted a series of consultations – as part of the National Dialogue – on the political reform of decentralization with stakeholders from civil society, academia and unions. This platform contributed to the drafting of a new local administration law, which seeks to revamp decentralization efforts by granting new powers and procedural requirements for Local, Executive and Governorate Councils.

While local authorities are progressively opening up, there is yet room to strengthen their relationship with the public and embed participation in the machinery of sub-national administrations. The following sections will review critical determinants for current practices by the three levels of government in Jordan to consult and engage stakeholders throughout the needs assessment process effectively.

Promoting stakeholder participation throughout the needs assessment process

Mainstreaming participation at all levels of the policymaking process helps ensure that outcomes respond to citizens' needs and expectations. Indeed, from the definition of policy priorities to their actual implementation and evaluation, stakeholder participation is a core element for the success of local policies (OECD, 2016) (See Figure 4.3). Paraguay, for example, has established a systematic process to engage with local communities in the creation of local development plans (See Box 4.1).

Figure 4.3. Stages of the Policy Making Cycle

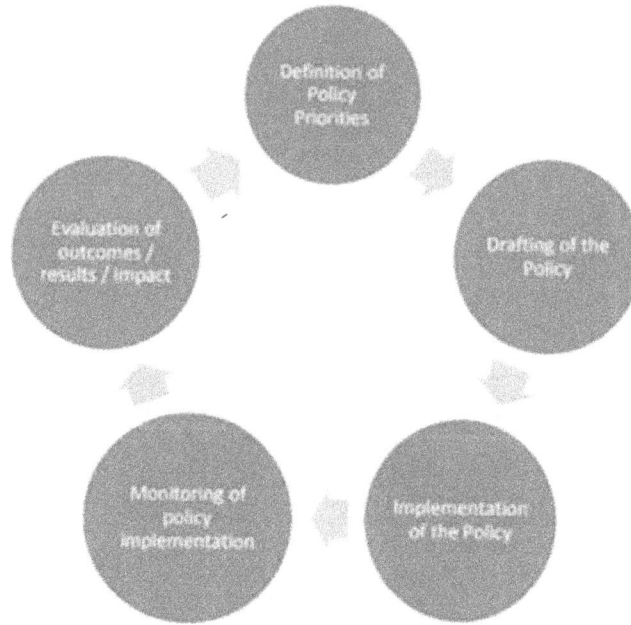

Source: OECD (2016), Open Government: The Global Context and the Way Forward, OECD

Box 4.1. Creating Local Development Plans with local communities in Paraguay

In 2014, the Ministry of Planning for Economic and Social Development (STP) in Paraguay, as one of the commitments made in their OGP National Action Plan, introduced a requirement for all municipalities to draft and present participatory Local Development Plans (LDPs) as a condition for receiving funds. The commitment mandated that municipalities adopted an open and participatory process to develop the LDPs: i.e. one that is transparent regarding the resources the municipality has and responsive to how the community believes they should be used.

This led to the development of 232 Municipal Development Councils (MDCs) across the country, designed to bring together local elected representatives, neighbourhood groups, businesses, representative civil society organisations, and municipal civil servants to develop LDPs that will improve public services, reduce corruption, ensure efficient management of public resources, and increase corporate responsibility. (Prior to the creation of the MDCs, the main actors taking the decisions at the local level were Mayors and Governors and decisions were likely to be made unilaterally.)

To support the implementation of this new way of working, the STP held regional meetings to inform the public about the establishment of MDCs. Municipality leaders, governors and staff were also trained on how to use a participatory process to draft LDPs and align them with the objectives of the National Development Plan–2030.

The city of Itauguá, home to more than 89,000 inhabitants and in one of Paraguay's most populated provinces with a mix of rural and urban areas, is one example of where the local authority, elected officials and civil society embraced the opportunities offered by this program.

For both the creation of the MDC, and for the subsequent development of the LDP for the city, a large scale participatory process was undertaken, which included substantial involvement from the general public.

The local authority started with an institutional diagnosis, which identified the strengths and weaknesses of the municipality. Sub-committees were then organised to develop proposals by issue area: Production; Health; Education; Childhood and Adolescence; Environment; Security; Infrastructure; Culture, Manufacturing and Sport; and Youth.

In an effort to consolidate the proposals in a way that both recognised the city's challenges and prioritised solutions, the MDC developed a participatory budgeting process, carried out through a citizens' assembly. At this event, the municipality shared information about the resources at the municipality's disposal, the proposals developed by the MDC sub-groups, its budget constraints, and the capacity of various departments and civil servants. Based on this information, residents of the city defined and prioritised which problems needed attention most urgently. Although the recommendations of the MDCs are not binding, the recommendation of the citizens' assembly in Itauguá were approved as part of the municipality budget for 2018.

Levels of engagement in the LDP process varied across the country, though officials note that their main challenge is keeping the MDCs running now that LDPs are in place. To help achieve this they have prepared support materials for developing monitoring plans for the process of implementation. These resources have been provided to all MDCs and include a "Matrix for Monitoring the Municipal Development Plan" to serve as a reporting tool to measure progress on commitments.

Source: Open Government Partnership (2018), Early Results of Open Government Partnership Initiatives, available online at: https://www.opengovpartnership.org/sites/default/files/OGP_Early-Results_Oct2018.pdf#

The iterative nature of the needs assessment process in Jordan represents an opportunity to include a variety of voices in the design of local policies and services. To maximize the value of stakeholder participation, initiatives ought to be embedded throughout all phases of defining local development projects and budgetary allocations (See Figure 4.4). As stated in Chapter 2, the current bottom-up approach consists of local and municipal authorities consulting citizens to develop a list of needs and priorities. This resulting needs manuals are shared with the Executive Council to develop the *Governorate Needs and Priorities Manual* with the help of GDUs. Once priorities are approved by the Governorate Council, the last stages of the process focus on the implementation of selected projects.

Figure 4.4. Stages of the Needs Assessment Process at the local level in Jordan

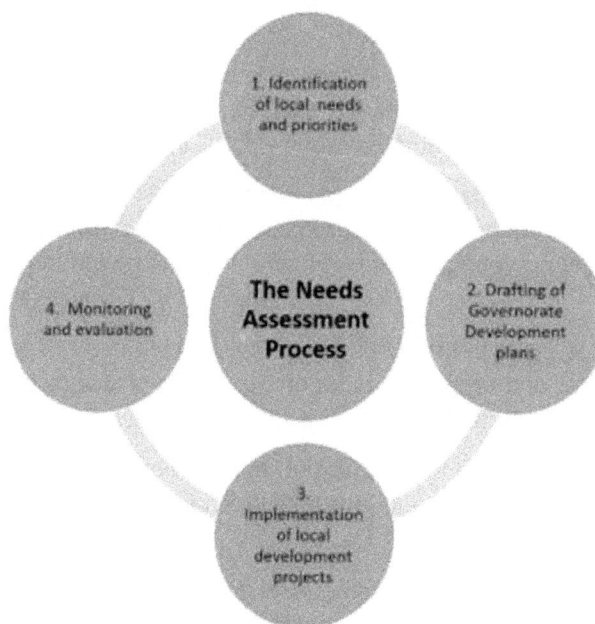

Source: Author's own work

Nevertheless, OECD interviews noted the existence of different degrees of engagement throughout the stages of the needs assessment process. In its initial phase, local and municipal authorities consult more actively with citizens. However, findings highlight that potential remains to make use of the benefits of stakeholder participation across the subsequent phases of consulting, drafting, implementing and evaluating local development plans. While progress has been achieved since 2018, it appears that participation remains understood as a one-off exercise to collect feedback rather than a partnership for co-creation with all interested parties.

Notably, the first stage of the identification of priorities is where citizens are most actively engaged at both local and municipal levels. Participation takes the form of open hearings, public consultations and an open-door policy from the mayor, such as the case of the Municipality of Salt. However, once the municipal document of needs is transferred to the Executive Council, findings from OECD interviews suggest that public validation processes and consultations by GDUs diminish significantly.

Local authorities in Jordan could therefore build on the existing participation activities to include Governorate stakeholders in a more systematic way. In particular, LDUs and GDUs could coordinate joint consultations at the Governorate level with citizens and municipalities on the transferred document of needs, for example, to increase ownership and buy-in. This would also help strengthen the relationship between citizens and Governorate Councils, and ensure that the needs lists continue to reflect local priorities as they are transferred from the Municipal to the Governorate levels.

Moreover, subnational authorities should seek to leverage the benefits of participation throughout the remaining stages of the needs assessment process. Opportunities for stakeholders to participate in the drafting and approval of Local Development Plans and budget allocations are generally low. As a manner of illustration, OECD survey data shows that only 20% of responding CSOs consider that stakeholders' contributions are reflected in the final plans, and 53% noted that this is unclear (see Figure 4.5). A second issue emphasizes the low level of ex post feedback, where 37% of CSO respondents, for example, were not able to submit public comments. Therefore, the establishment of validation and review processes could be considered for the final list of priorities before the approval of local plans through required quarterly hearings or evaluation reports. Creating meaningful opportunities for citizens to participate in the co-creation of plans could help address growing scepticism around the needs assessment process.

Figure 4.5. Share of CSOs noting whether they feel the contributions made by stakeholders are considered in the needs assessment process

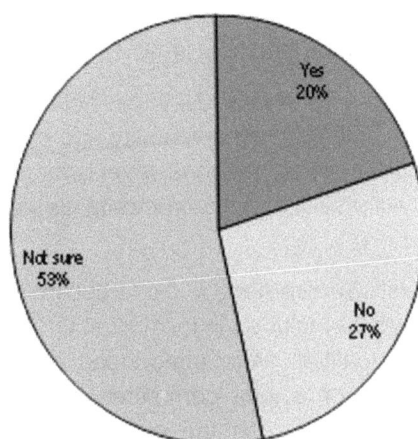

Source: OECD (2019), Questionnaire for Civil Society Organizations: Stakeholder participation in Jordan's needs assessment process.

In parallel, the engagement with contractors in charge of implementing local development projects is central to their effectiveness and sustainability. During OECD workshops, government officials emphasized that interactions with local partners are conducted on an ad-hoc basis. This in turn affects the ability of partners to implement local projects, primarily due to the low levels of information sharing and involvement in the feasibility assessment of projects. Therefore, there is an opportunity to strengthen the involvement of business contractors from the earlier stages of the needs assessment process.

Enhancing opportunities for consultation and engagement at the local level

The creation of new participation opportunities alone, however, does not necessarily lead to an equivalent increase in the quality and legitimacy of policy decisions. Meaningful opportunities to participate call for citizens to have a greater role in the co-design of local policies and services. Indeed, new spaces for local participation need to be accompanied by the systematic inclusion of a diverse group of stakeholders, going beyond the usual suspects (OECD, 2016; OECD, 2017a).

At the national level, Jordan has achieved progress in promoting the participation of stakeholders in the framework of the country's open government agenda. The development process of Jordan's fourth OGP

National Action Plan (2018 - 2020), led by the Open Government Unit in the Ministry of Planning and International Cooperation, was the most inclusive and consultative to date, with over 2,034 Facebook engagements (likes and comments); 269 participants in meetings and consultation sessions; and 145 responses to the opinion poll and call for public comments. Relevant for the decentralization reform, the third and fourth OGP National Action Plans include commitments focused on enhancing partnerships and dialogue with civil society and fostering national dialogues for political reform, further highlighting the relevance of this topic in Jordan. As these efforts have mainly focused at the national level, however, there is an opportunity to leverage the opportunities presented by decentralization to further embed the principles of stakeholder participation at the local level. As in the case of Tunisia (see Box 4.2), OGP commitments could target a selection of governorates to implement participation initiatives around the decentralization process. More broadly, the country could consider expanding its current collaboration to join the OGP Local Programme.

Box 4.2. Implementing local OGP commitments in Tunisia

Since 2011, over 332 local level commitments have been made within the OGP National Action Plans of 60 countries around the world. For example, Tunisia recently developed its first commitment to embed the principles of open government at the local level.

Specifically, commitment 11 of Tunisia's Third OGP National Action Plan calls for the implementation of initiatives to promote transparency, integrity, accountability and stakeholder participation at the local level. The aim of expanding the scope to the sub-national level is for municipalities to develop initiatives that are in line with the region's characteristics and requirements, as well as rendering the administration more accessible to citizens.

To ensure its relevance, the Tunisian Government, in close collaboration with civil society, opened a call to select 12 Municipalities that will be included in local level OGP activities. Out of 73 applications received, the twelve selected municipalities were announced on October 2019. Activities will be coordinated through regular meetings of a joint committee comprising of representatives of the administration at the municipality level and representatives of the region's residents.

Source: Open Government Partnership, Tunisia (2019) Call for applications for the selection of municipalities to implement initiatives devoting the OGP at the local level, available online at: http://www.ogptunisie.gov.tn/en/?p=1762

With the election of Governorate and Local Councils in 2017, sub-national authorities have also began a process to engage citizens in the design of local development plans. A range of participation practices to collect needs are carried out mostly by LDUs, including the organization of hearings, consultations and online surveys. These practices, however, focus primarily on consulting citizens on needs rather than involving them in the broader co-design and co-production of local policies and services. Moreover, the scale and representativeness of these initiatives tend to vary across large and small governorates and are still conducted on an ad-hoc basis.

As a result, participation levels since the first needs assessment in 2018 remain generally low. A perception survey conducted in 2018 identified that 46% of Jordanians noted no change in the number of opportunities to participate in the definition of priorities for their municipality, followed by 28% that perceived even fewer instances (International Republic Institute, 2018). These findings align with OECD survey data, where less than half of responding CSOs (12 out of 30) have participated in the needs assessment process. Public servants in their majority attribute the "lack of trust", "lack of awareness of CSOs on their role within the decentralization process" and "lack of communication" as the main reasons for the low involvement of stakeholders in this process (see Figure 4.6). OECD interviews also found a general lack of data collected on the degree and level of participation of citizens, civil society and businesses in the needs assessment process. In line with the section above, the Government could benefit from instilling a mechanism that documents levels of participation to inform the design of future activities and better showcase results.

Figure 4.6. Main Challenges in Engaging Stakeholders in the Needs Assessment Process

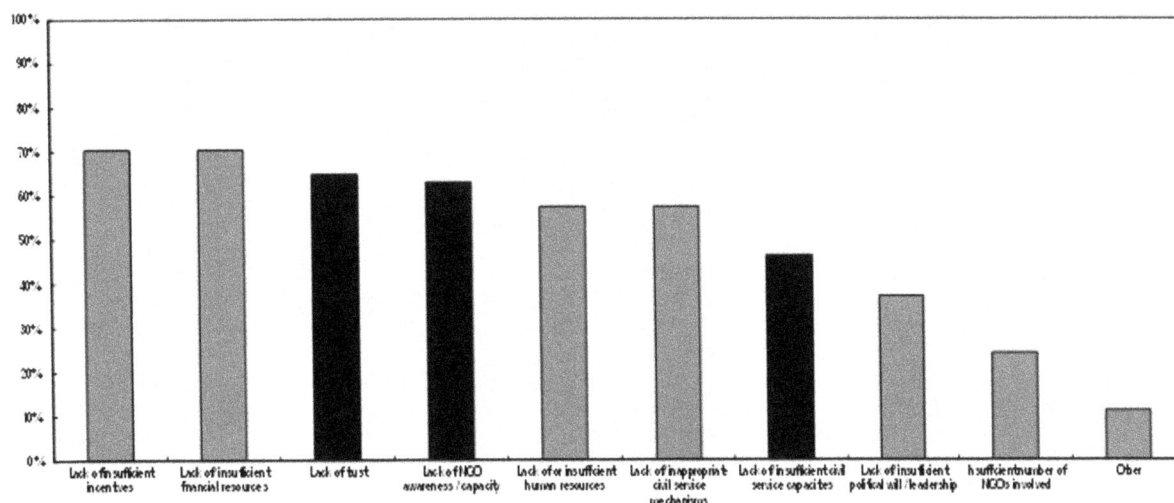

Source: OECD (2019) Questionnaire for Sub-national Authorities: Stakeholder participation in Jordan's needs assessment process

An exception where participation has indeed been documented to inform policy reform in the framework of decentralization is through Jordan's National Dialogue. Its 2019 edition consisted of 43 sessions with a total of 1,568 participants from civil society, academia and government across the 12 Governorates. While the National Dialogue has been an effective platform to bring about changes to the decentralization process, the Government of Jordan could institutionalize this mechanism and increase its reach through the formation of sub-committees with civil society, academia and public authorities from large and small governorates equally.

More broadly, the Government of Jordan should focus on increasing the representativeness and procedural effectiveness of participation initiatives, with a focus on transitioning from consultation toward engagement. In line with practices from OECD member and partner countries (see Table 4.1), Jordan could make use of a range of participation mechanisms according to the needs of local communities. Making use of novel forms of stakeholder participation, such as citizen panels and deliberative processes, could promote new mechanisms to engage the public in a more meaningful way (see Box 4.3 on the experience of Citizen Panels in Melbourne). To maximize these benefits, however, institutionalizing participation initiatives would help expand the engagement and increase the representativeness of stakeholders. In this respect, the current reform of the Local Administration Law presents a valuable opportunity to consider the inclusion of provisions regarding the institutionalisation of these practices across subnational entities.

Table 4.1. Overview of stakeholder participation practices in OECD countries

Name of the initiative	Goal	Nature of topics discussed	Organiser	Duration/number of participants
21st Century Townhall Meeting	Advise decision makers through the use of modern technology	Mainly local issues (e.g. communal development)	Municipalities, agencies	1 day/ 500-5 000 people
Citizen Forum	Strengthen democratic competencies, initiate debate in society	Discussions on regional, national and transnational issues	Private foundations (to date)	Various weeks/300-10 000 people
Participatory budgeting	Citizens participate in budget decisions	Setting of priorities for expenditures and consolidation of local and communal budgets	Local politicians, local government	Various months (up to 10 000 people)
Citizen Panel	Advise decision makers	Feedback for politicians and service providers, long-term change in public perception	Local politicians, local government, other stakeholders	3-4 years (up to 4 surveys each year)/ 500-2 500 people
Citizens' Council	Influence debates in society, advise decision makers	Communal development and local topics	Local politicians, local government, clubs, enterprises	2-day meetings in various months/ small groups of 8-12 people
Deliberative Polling	Information transfer, deliberation	Wide range of topics, ranging from local to transnational issues	Political decision makers	Various weeks/300-500 people
Consensus Conference	Exchange among experts and laypersons	Controversial topics of public interest, local to transnational questions	Agencies	3 days (+2 preparation weekends) /10-30 people
National Issues Forum	Information transfer, acquisition of competencies	Different topics linked to public organisation of local to national relevance	Municipalities, schools, universities and other educational institutions	1-2 days/10-20 people
Open Space Conference	Brainstorm and develop new ideas	Potentially any topic which requires a new or creative idea	Enterprises, clubs, agencies, communal agencies, educational institutions, church,.	1-3 days/ flexible (10-2 000 people)
Planning for Reality	Reorganise common spaces	Projects in urban planning	Local politicians, local government, similar institutions	Various months/ flexible
Planning Cell	Integrate citizens' knowledge into planning decisions	Problems of local and regional planning (urban planning, infrastructure)	Local politicians, local government, similar institutions	2-4 days (flexible, max. 25 people per planning cell)
Scenario technique	Balance different future scenarios	Anticipation of future developments and issuing recommendations on different topics (local to transnational)	Enterprises, clubs, institutions, local government, educational institutions, church ,etc.	1-3 days/flexible (25-250 people, max. 30 people per group)
World Café	Use of collective intelligence	Potentially any topic which requires a new or creative	Enterprises, clubs,	Flexible (3 hours to 2 days)/flexible (12-1

		idea	institutions, local government, educational institutions, church etc.	200 people)
Future workshop	Develop creative approaches to solving complex challenges, and common perspectives on the future	Long-term changes and ways to influence processes and projects	Municipalities, institutions, organisations, clubs, etc.	2-3 days/ flexible (max. 25 people per group)

Source: OECD (2019), Open Government in Argentina, OECD Public Governance Reviews, OECD Publishing, Paris, https://doi.org/10.1787/1988ccef-en.

Box 4.3. The City of Melbourne's Citizen Panel

In 2014, the City of Melbourne Council faced the challenge of balancing its budget, within a context of a growing need for infrastructure investment, a changing population, and an $800-900m (AUD) budget gap between what council had promised to deliver and its capacity to fund it on current budget settings.

In preparing for its 10 Year Financial Plan, the Council took an open policy making approach and sought advice from the public to help determine how projects should be funded and which ones should be prioritised, while retaining an overall goal to "remain one of the world's most liveable cities, [and maintain a] strong financial position."

After a wide-ranging process of open consultation with the public, the government established the People's Panel (45 residents randomly selected to be representative of the city' population). Meeting for daylong sessions on alternate Saturdays over 2-3 months, the panel engaged in a process of learning about the issues (including the open and transparent assessment of the Council's budget, revenue streams and investment plans), weighting up priorities and options and developing recommendations.

These recommendations, which were assessed as being realistic and "highly implementable", included:

- Supporting the sales of non-core assets to reduce the council's property portfolio;
- Increasing funding to address climate change;
- A 5 year plan for introducing more bicycle lanes in the city;
- Decreasing expenditure on new capital works by 10% over the next 10 years;
- Raising local taxes paid to the council by up to 2.5% per annum for 10 years.

The final 10 Year Financial Plan produced by the City of Melbourne Council was heavily influenced by the People's Panel, with 10 of the 11 recommendations made broadly accepted. This plan not only solved the budget deficit but also increased panel members' sense of satisfaction with the city's direction: evaluations showed that 96% of them highly rated their experience as part of the People's Panel and had "higher levels of confidence in the City of Melbourne".

Source: City of Melbourne (2019), Participate Melbourne, accessed on 5 May 2019, https://participate.melbourne.vic.gov.au/10yearplan

Building mechanisms to support stakeholder participation at the local level

The successful implementation of stakeholder participation initiatives depends largely on the existence of adequate institutional structures. To that end, the lack of standards and mechanisms (i.e. guides, manuals, protocols) is one of the main bottlenecks to institutionalizing stakeholder participation in Jordan. According to OECD survey data, the majority of government respondents noted insufficient incentives (70%) and the lack of public service tools and mechanisms (57%) as two key barriers in involving stakeholders in the needs assessment process. As previously mentioned, tools and guidance needed at the local level should be backed up by a comprehensive legal framework for decentralization that acknowledges the important role of stakeholder participation. This lack of institutional mechanisms, however, has implications for both government authorities and CSOs alike.

For public authorities, establishing and clarifying mechanisms at the three levels of government will be key for public servants to integrate stakeholders in local activities. Findings from OECD workshops highlighted a lack of standards on how to go about engaging with stakeholders. This challenge was particularly emphasized by LDUs, were capacity and resources to carry out consultations is often lacking.

A first step to mitigating these challenges could therefore include the assignment of clear institutional responsibilities for local, municipal and governorate actors on stakeholder participation initiatives. This could be followed by a series of capacity building activities to support these functions, and the development of a set of consultation guidelines on, for example:

1. How to engage stakeholders at each stage of the Needs Assessment Process and mapping the process and opportunities for participation;
2. How to ensure representativeness and diversity of stakeholders; inclusivity throughout all stages of the process; ensure gender sensitivity; the development of criteria to map stakeholders;
3. How to validate inputs by citizens; and
4. How to communicate throughout the process and about results to maximize impact in a way that is easily accessible in a clear, complete, timely, reliable and re-usable format.

For CSOs and citizens, furthermore, mechanisms are also needed to ensure that they have not just the opportunity, but the capacity to participate in the development of local development plans. OECD data shows that while 60% of responding CSOs received capacity building related to the needs assessment process, these trainings were carried out by other national or local CSOs (89%) or donor organizations (39%). To this end, the MoLA could adopt a larger role in providing these trainings to increase CSO capacity and engagement, as well as ensure that trainings are provided across the country. Capacity building modules could also be designed to raise the awareness on any future legal reforms, as well as to provide civil society with the appropriate tools, guidelines and skills to leverage their role throughout the decentralization process. Topics could include identifying policy priorities, evaluating performance indicators, using and re-using open government data, submitting information requests and social media engagement, amongst others.

Solely establishing mechanisms, however, will not ensure their uptake. More broadly, the country should seek to promote a culture of openness and continuous learning at the sub-national level. To that end, a multi-stakeholder platform could be designed to promote an open dialogue between government representatives, civil society, private sector and citizens from different local communities. This platform could build on efforts from the National Dialogue to share best practices, reflect on lessons learned, identify common challenges and promote participation throughout the decentralization process. Such a platform could take the form of a local innovation laboratory to build a community of practice, as in the case of Santalab in the Santa Fe Province in Argentina (see Box 4.4); it could also take the form of an informal network of mayors focused on increasing coordination and cross-fertilizing best practices within governorates.

> **Box 4.4. Promoting citizen-driven innovation at the local level: The case of Santalab**
>
> Santalab is an open citizen innovation laboratory in the province of Santa Fe, Argentina. Santalab serves as both a virtual and physical space where citizens, public authorities and businesses can meet and work together. Santalab carries out three different types of activities – namely outreach, training and prototyping activities – targeting specific audiences. Through its outreach activities, the lab aims to raise awareness of key local level issues and promote a space for community engagement. Santalab also provides training and co-creation activities through free workshops aimed at building the capacity of key players to contribute to the development of local policies and the design of services. It also promotes a space for experimentation and prototyping aimed at embedding citizen innovation at the core of the machinery of the local administration.
>
> *Source:* OECD (2019), Open Government in Argentina, OECD Public Governance Reviews, OECD Publishing, Paris, https://doi.org/10.1787/1988ccef-en.

Recommendations

With the rapid transformations brought by the decentralization reform, sub-national authorities are adopting initiatives to inform, consult and engage stakeholders in the needs assessment process. Acting on the lessons learned from two needs cycles will be essential to establish new partnerships with citizens. Broadly, a meaningful and open relationship calls for sub-national authorities in Jordan to scale up efforts toward changing the role of citizens from passive receivers to that of partners in the co-creation of local policies and services.

Bridging the divide between sub-national governments and citizens is a primary objective of the decentralization reform. Despite the progress achieved in terms of opening the decision making process for local development plans, there is room to leverage participation opportunities throughout all the stages of the needs assessment process. Ensuring effective stakeholder participation will also require the promotion of stakeholder diversity, in particular of under-represented groups. In parallel, efforts will entail building necessary structures to support stakeholder participation at the local level, through skills and best practice sharing.

To this end, the Government of Jordan could consider the below recommendations:

- Leverage current OGP activities to promote the principles of stakeholder participation at the local level through the development of commitments in selected governorates. The administration could also consider including a commitment in the next OGP action plan aimed at supporting participation at the local level. More broadly, the country could consider expanding its current collaboration to engage several municipalities in the OGP Local Programme.
- Increase the scope of activities for citizens to participate throughout all the stages of the needs assessment process, in particular at the drafting and validating phases of local development plans. Participation mechanisms could also be used to share updates and outcomes of the needs assessment plans and how these supported the approved local development plan.
- LDUs and GDUs could coordinate joint consultations with citizens and municipalities on the transferred document of needs, for example, to increase ownership and buy-in.
- Assign clear institutional responsibilities for stakeholder participation for local, municipal and governorate actors, including LDUs and GDUs.

- Develop and adopt a mechanism for governorate and municipal entities to document the levels of participation in local activities. Measuring the impact of stakeholder participation initiatives will not only help inform the design of future activities but also showcase results to the highest political levels.

- Establish participation initiatives that move beyond sole consultation to assign a more direct and meaningful role for citizens in the co-creation of local policies. The Government of Jordan could thus consider adopting engagement practices such as citizen panels, planning cells and other deliberative processes.

- Consider the inclusion of provisions to institutionalise consultations and other participation related initiatives as part of the ongoing reform of the Local Administration Law. This would not only clarify the mandate for municipal and governorate actors, but also help consolidate implementation mechanisms, promote their adoption and reiterate the values of stakeholder participation beyond solely the Renaissance Plan.

- Develop a set of consultation guidelines aimed at all government stakeholders focused on:
    1. How to engage stakeholders at each stage of the needs assessment process and map processes and opportunities for participation.
    2. How to ensure representativeness and diversity of stakeholders and establish criteria to identify stakeholders.
    3. How to validate inputs by citizens.
    4. How to communicate throughout the process and about results to maximize impact.

- Develop a set of criteria or standards on how citizens can develop their list of needs. These standards could be included in the manual shared to municipal stakeholders by national authorities and be widely disseminated.

- Leverage the role of MoLA to design and carry out more capacity building modules aimed at providing civil society organizations with the appropriate tools, guidelines and skills to leverage their important role throughout the decentralization process. These workshops could raise awareness around key issues by focusing on current gaps, such as identifying policy priorities, evaluating performance indicators, engaging and communicating with public officials, among others.

- Expand on the National Dialogue to develop a formal multi-stakeholder platform to promote an open dialogue between government representatives, civil society, private sector and citizens from different local communities. The platform could take the form of an innovation lab or an informal network of mayors to share best practices, reflect on lessons learned, identify common challenges and solutions to promote stakeholder participation throughout the needs assessment process.

References

Arab Barometer (2019), Jordan Country Report, https://www.arabbarometer.org/countries/jordan/

International Republican Institute (2018), *Public Opinion Survey: Residents of Jordan*, Center for Insights in Survey Research, available online at: https://www.iri.org/resource/jordan-poll-reveals-low-trust-government-increasing-economic-hardship

Mahadin E., Binda C. & Khasawneh M. (2018), *Legal Review of the Jordanian Decentralization Law*, issued by Karak Castle Center for Consultations and Training.

OECD (2017a), *The OECD Recommendation of the Council on Open Government*, OECD Legal Instruments, Paris, https://legalinstruments.oecd.org/public/doc/359/d5392da9-6aa6-4647-b266-2e37694c497f.htm

OECD (2017b), *Contextualising decentralisation reform and open government in Jordan*, in Towards a New Partnership with Citizens: Jordan's Decentralisation Reform, OECD Publishing, Paris, https://doi.org/10.1787/9789264275461-5-en.

OECD (2017c), *Organisation and functions at the centre of government: Centre Stage II*, survey response report, internal document.

OECD (2016), *Open Government: The Global Context and the Way Forward*, OECD Publishing, Paris, https://doi.org/10.1787/9789264268104-en.

Note

[1] Municipal: to a moderate degree (37%) + large degree (15%); Governorate councils: to a moderate degree (33%) + large degree (11%); Parliament: to a moderate degree (11%) + large degree (2%)